HUMAN DEVELOPMENT *and the* THEATER *of* EVERYDAY LIFE

HUMAN DEVELOPMENT *and the* THEATER *of* EVERYDAY LIFE

DAVID THOMAS, PHD

Ethics for Self, Workplace, and Society

Langdon Street Press • Maitland

For information on the Ethics of Human Development Training Program, contact David Thomas, PhD at dtec@cox.net.

Langdon Street Press
2301 Lucien Way #415
Maitland, FL 32751
407.339.4217
www.langdonstreetpress.com

ISBN-13: 978-1-63505-393-7
LCCN: 2016956727

Distributed by Itasca Books

Cover image: *"Golden Rai*n" by Russian-American artist, Victor Nizovtsev

Cover Design by James Arneson

Printed in the United States of America

For my parents

Table of Contents

Acknowledgments

It has taken me a long time to write this book. In a sense, it began in 1983 with the development of "The Five Levels" schematic and then later, in 1992 and over the years since, with the development and testing of the Ethics of Human Development Training Program. There are many people to thank.

For their support, feedback, and encouragement during the development of the ethics training program, I would like to thank Doug Paterson, Don Jennings, Jay Williamson, Terry Kempf, David Shrader, Dan Wilkins, Keith and Ocoee Miller, Gordon Becker, Phil Minkin, John Thomas, Beth Garrett, Charlie Hill, Daniel Dancer, R. Ross Gipple, Nancy Kelly, Richard Goldstein, Thomas Reed, Warren Zweiback, Jon Levin, John Miller, William Tuttle, Donald Stilson, and Paula Ziegman.

In addition, there have been a number of individuals in leadership positions within their respective organizations who believed in the value of the ethics training program (then called "The Ethics of Choice Training Program") and who invited it into their organizations. Without their belief in the content of the program and their willingness to experiment with it inside their organizations, the program could not have developed. In this regard, I wish to thank Richard and Phyllis Gilliland, Jane Matheson, Cheryl Doherty, Pat Cavill, Dean Fixsen, Karen Blasé, Gene Klein, Bob Vodica, Scot Adams, Vicki Maca, Jeffrey Johnson, Jay Williamson, Howard Shrier, Kathleen Doyle-Linden, Sonny Foster, and Judy Mallory.

There is a group of individuals with whom I have been in dialogue on the issues addressed in this book for many years. They have been teachers, fellow travelers, members—though we may never have talked about it in this way—of what I considered my research group. In this regard, I would like to acknowledge and thank Bill Boykin, Frank L. Lang, Susan McBeth, Wilford Martinez, Dan and Jesse Luna Sr., Dan Martinez, Dan Luna Jr. and Paula Leek, Chuck Luna, Ray Foster, Donald Stilson, Johann

Stoyva, Thomas Budzynski, Bill Porter, Keith and Ocoee Miller, Daniel Dancer, Richard Goldstein and Andrea Bossak, Rick Dangel, Michael Herzmark, Phil Minkin, William Tuttle, Don Mayberger, John Bowden, and Stan Herd. That group goes back to graduate school and before.

Over the years since, there have been others with whom the same dialogue and friendship evolved. They, along with those mentioned above, have taught me a great deal, and I am extremely grateful to them. In this regard, I wish to thank Jeff Edelman and Sue Parkison, David Shrader, Bob Clark, R. Ross Gipple, Dan and Pam Daly, Beth Caldwell, Gordon Becker, Guy Cornwell, Don and Betty Green, Dan and Rebecca Boylan, Dean Fixsen and Karen Blasé, Robert and Karen Slovek, Jon and Jackie Okun, Sandy Aquila, Nancy and Jek Kelly, Mike McLarney, Bob Georgi, Terry Kempf, Jay Williamson, Jon Levin, Doug Paterson, Verne Varona, Ward Peters, Warren Jabali and Mary Beasley, Len Trower-Mfuasi, Alex Ellison, Al Smith, Kennie Denmon, Robert C. Peters, Mike Saklar, Scot Adams, Del Bomberger, and James R. Thele.

In the writing of this book, I particularly want to thank Doug Paterson, Scot Adams, Bill Porter, R. Ross Gipple, Len Trower-Mfuasi, Dan Luna Jr., Chuck Luna, L. Keith Miller, Don Seten, Kathleen Magor, Blythe Hurley, and Laura Lavington for reading drafts of this manuscript and offering their comments and suggestions. This was invaluable to me. Similarly, I want to thank Derek Miller, Bill Lukash, and Nataliya Lys for their assistance with the images used in the book. Special thanks to Victor Nizovtsev for permitting the use of his painting for the book's cover, and special thanks as well to Cynthia McBride of the McBride Gallery, Annapolis, Maryland, for her assistance in this matter.

There are a number of writers and thinkers who have influenced this work. Though I came across them at different times in my life, all moved me with the clarity of their thought and the humanity embedded in their work. I want to mention, in particular, the following: R. Buckminster Fuller, John David Garcia, E. F. Schumacher, Ken Wilber, Bruce Wilshire, James Carse, Ernest Becker, B. F. Skinner, Eckert Tolle, Steven Hayes, Montrose Wolf, William Tuttle, and L. Keith Miller.

I want to extend my heartfelt thanks to R. Ross Gipple for his belief in this work and his kind support in making the completion of this book possible.

In many respects, I wrote this book for my family. It is dedicated to my parents, Burt and Betty Thomas, but with my extended family, my children, and their families very much in mind. Dwain and Lora Dean Smith, Louise Hawkins, Beth Garrett and her long time friend, Blake Elliott, Nick and Katie Lane and their children, Thomas and Nickolas, Luke and Lacy Garrett and Luke's son, Tyson, and John and Ann Thomas and their children, David, Laura, Jane, and Mary Kate. All have given me their time, love, and support throughout my life. And my daughters and their families, Blake Thomas and Alistair Wandesforde, and their children Louise, Gordon, Freddy, and Vera, and Chesley Thomas and Matt Kudlacz, and their children, Kate and Johnny, about whom I cannot say enough. They have enriched my life immeasurably.

Finally, I want to thank my life partner, Paula Ziegman. What she has contributed to this work (and to me) is difficult to put into words. My worldview is enlarged because of her. She has my enduring love and respect. I thank her in particular for the support and understanding she extended to me during the writing of this book and for the ongoing dialogue that enriched many sections of the book and continues to enrich my life.

—David Thomas
January 2018

Preface

"For even higher than the life of art is the art of life. And ethics is the lore of the art of life."[1]

—Will Durant
The Mansions of Philosophy

Roy Rogers was America's favorite cowboy. When he died (1998), people looked back to a time when he filled the big screen and, later, came into America's homes with his Saturday morning television show. This was the 1950s. Fathers had returned from the war and were back at work. Mothers were raising children and creating neighborhoods. The nation was being reborn.

Roy was a part of that time. According to one commentator, Roy and his films filled a vacuum of which most people were unaware: In the Westerns of those days, no one saw any blood. Guns fired. Fists flew. The bad guys fell. The flesh, however, never tore. These were B movies starring a singing cowboy, but mostly, and above all, they were morality plays providing far more guidance to children of troubled families than most people might imagine.[2]

How are we to view life? It is a question worth considering because how we view life can affect our approach to it. For Picasso, life was a miracle, pure and simple. A marvel to behold. For the writer Conrad Aiken, it was a comic pilgrimage, an attempt to get somewhere—wherever that somewhere was—through efforts both heartfelt and bungling. And then there are those, too many to credit, for whom life is a dream, full of meaning, perhaps, but with a will and logic all its own.

For the purposes of this book, life will be viewed as a morality play (not unlike one of Roy's movies) with each of us cast as actors in the play. This view emphasizes choice—the role of choice both in shaping character and in moving the play along. The play itself is assumed to be an ensemble piece, making available a meaningful if not prominent role to anyone who wants one. To layer this view, it is further assumed that each of us is in our own morality play and that it lasts a lifetime; and, at another level, that there is the larger morality play that is the human drama itself. In both cases, the presumption is that the script is not written ahead of time but, instead, is written as we go.

If we view life in this way, then the topic of ethics—the lore that guides us—necessarily follows. To be clear, however, the ethics discussed in this book are not business ethics, corporate ethics, medical ethics, or environmental ethics, as important as these topics are. Instead, the focus here is on the ethics of human development, the ethics that further our development as persons. The focus is on the ethics likely to foster the psychological integration or wholeness needed for what Durant (in our opening quote) may have meant by the art of life—i.e., a life rich with purpose, creatively lived and deeply felt, a life of benefit to others, as well as to one's self.[3]

At the heart of the discussion to follow is the notion of ethics as human logic, the logic (and rules of conduct) by which we educate, mature, and enlighten ourselves.[4] This notion is discussed throughout the book and is given detail in the descriptions of the ethics themselves. However, that discussion can be foreshadowed by a return to Roy and to the presumption of life as morality play—miracle, dream, pilgrimage, yes—but morality play as well.

When the character Roy played in the movies righted wrong, the community benefited. But so, too, did Roy. He became wiser, more conscious, more capable of dealing with similar situations in the future. His persistence on behalf of what he believed was required of him shaped and further strengthened his capacity to act on principle. That is ethics as human logic. The self serves the whole but not generally and over the long run at the expense of the self. "The gift is to the giver and comes back most to him [or her] . . . It cannot fail"[5]—that was Whitman's way of putting it, and that will be a central theme throughout this book: ethical conduct for the sake of the other and for the common good, but for the sake of one's own development, as well.

Finally, there is no presumption of self-sacrifice in the discussion that follows, not in the deepest sense—only expanded self-interest. What motivates us to behave in accord with the ethics discussed here is presumed inherent: namely, our desire for greater clarity, our desire to know who we are and what purpose we might serve, our desire to attain a maturity or self-mastery that might be termed "enlightened."[6]

There are five parts to this book:

Part I: Human Development and the Yellow Brick Road. Part I provides a map of the developmental possibilities available to each of us as human beings, from the innocence and dependence of the infant to the wisdom and independence of the fully mature adult. These levels of development are described along with a brief overview of humandevelopment in order to show the direction in which we move when we conduct ourselves in accord with the ethics of human development. The ethics themselves are presented in Part II, but the developmental road they help us travel is described in Part I.

Part II: Human Logic and the Ethics of Human Development. Part II presents the ethics of human development, the ethics that give body and detail to the notion of human logic. In explaining these ethics, the focus is on our life in organizations. The presumption in Part II is twofold: first, that we are involved with organizations throughout our lives, beginning (and ending, perhaps) with the family, but also including work, school, and community; and second, that how we operate in these organizations dramatically affects the development of the organizations in question and our own development, as well.

Part III: Dilemmas from Everyday Life. Part III provides examples of situations in everyday life that present us with ethical dilemmas. These dilemmas offer developmental possibility. They are choice points providing a measure of ethical strength while also offering an opportunity to exercise and deepen that strength. The development of heart, mind, and will—in other words, our development as persons—depends on the learning opportunities that even the smallest of these dilemmas offers.

Part IV: The Ideas with Which We See. Part IV focuses on "the ideas with which we see"; the ideas/values with which we organize and define our experience. This topic is critical because the ideas/values we have (and hold) in mind go a long way toward determining how we will respond to the everyday dilemmas that come our way. Thus, in Part IV we discuss the management of the self, i.e., what we can do to affect the likelihood that we will behave ethically and thus, make choices that raise (rather than lower) the "center of gravity" in ourselves, in our organizations, and in society.

Part V: The Theater of Change. Finally, Part V provides a brief overview of the training program developed to teach the ethics of human development and then continues with a discussion of the larger forces affecting development. Concerning those forces, there is, on the one hand, the fear that encourages us to settle for the current version of who and what we are, choosing withdrawal from life's challenges rather than the possibility of personal growth. And, on the other hand, there is the "ontological longing" for greater self-realization. In Part V, the self is defined by its effects on others and by its effects on the physical and biological environment. By that definition, the role of ethics is made central to the development of both self and society.

What is the largest, most consequential game we can play, the greatest adventure to which we can commit ourselves? This is a question we sometimes consider when we feel relaxed and safe enough to do so, or when our own interior development permits us to see through the limited nature of the cause or sphere we have been serving. For many, the answer is human development—one's own and that of others. Certainly there is no front on which this "game" cannot be played, including government, education, business, the family, and always the self.

But how is this game played? In his Pulitzer Prize–winning book *The Denial of Death*, Ernest Becker wrote, "People create the reality they need in order to discover themselves."[7] Perhaps here we have a clue. We have created the reality in which we find ourselves—its inhumanities, its imbalances, its glorious aspects. And by observing the reality we have created, by seeing the impact we have (and have had) on others and on the physical and biological environment, we give ourselves feedback on who and what we are. We discover ourselves in what we observe. And with this discovery—this feedback—comes the opportunity to make more of our selves. It is a developmental process, one of self-recognition, self-assessment, and, if need be, self-change (providing we have the will for it). And now, with reality as it is (the disparities and inequalities so severe, the need for creative problem-solving so great), we discover ourselves reflected in the large and complex dilemmas of our time.

The ethics of human development (and the program designed to teach them) is one initiative among many created in response to the dilemmas we now face and, in a sense, have always faced. Its emphasis is on the evolving self and on the benefits an evolved and evolving self can bring to others. The view presented in what follows is this: A person's capacities are expanded and his understanding deepened by conduct in accord with the ethics of human development. If more and more individuals, organizations, and institutions can anchor themselves to these ethics (whatever else they are doing to improve themselves), then a more creative culture can emerge—more creative because the individuals comprising the culture are more creative (and less destructive). When this is understood and acted upon, then everyday life becomes a theater wherein a play of factors provides a continuous opportunity for personal growth and meaningful change.

"Higher than the life of art is the art of life"—and what is the art of life? It is, from the point of view of this book, the meeting and enriching of what is given with the best that is in us. To practice this art, as with any art, is to get better at it. Our capacity is expanded because, increasingly, we know what we are doing. Our understanding of who we are and what we can do meets with a growing knowledge of what is required for art's sake. Life is made more beautiful in this way, and more fulfilling, and the small world of which we are a part, if only by degree, is improved. That is the theme of this book: Through the ethical comes self-realization. Conduct in accord with human logic matures us, makes us wise, and makes the world more humane. The morality play that is life on this planet is moved forward, with the development brought about in ourselves certain to benefit others.

Part I

Human Development and the Yellow Brick Road

> "In the whole of philosophy, there is no subject in greater disarray than ethics. Anyone asking the professors of ethics for the bread of guidance or how to conduct himself, will receive not even a stone but just a torrent of 'opinions.' With very few exceptions, they embark upon an investigation into ethics without any prior clarification of the purpose of human life on Earth. It is obviously impossible to decide what is good or bad, right or wrong, virtuous or evil, without an idea of purpose: Good for what? To raise the question of purpose has been called 'the naturalistic fallacy'—virtue is its own reward! None of the great teachers of mankind would have been satisfied with such an evasion. If a thing is said to be good but no one can tell me what it is good for, how can I be expected to take any interest in it? If our guide, our annotated Map of Life, cannot show us where The Good is situated and how it can be reached, it is worthless."[1]
>
> —E. F. Schumacher
> *A Guide for the Perplexed*

This book is an attempt to address the disarray to which Schumacher refers in the above passage. A "map of life" is presented and on it is shown "where the Good is situated." It is situated, according to the map, in the direction of our fullest possible maturity as human beings. Purpose is found in the pursuit of that maturity, a maturity that values human development first and foremost and that serves life overall.

TWO ASSUMPTIONS

Two assumptions operate throughout this book. The first is that we want for ourselves the realization of our full potential as human beings. As noted psychologist Carl Rogers put it, "There is in every organism, at whatever level, an underlying flow of movement toward constructive fulfillment of its inherent possibilities."[2] That is the first assumption: we want for ourselves the "constructive fulfillment of inherent possibilities." The second assumption is that ethical conduct facilitates that fulfillment.

Most of us, of course, never realize the fulfillment of our inherent possibilities. We lack the stamina for it, or the discipline. And we may lack the support we need from others. According to ethicist John David Garcia, in order to achieve our full developmental potential, we must receive unconditional love from at least one other person in our life.[3] Without the honoring we experience when we are loved unconditionally, we are perhaps less able to conclude that we are valuable, less able to honor ourselves by persisting in the pursuit of inherent possibilities when the going gets tough.

And while unconditional love from at least one other person is fundamental to our development (presuming Garcia is correct), it is also helpful to live within a culture that values human development. It is extremely helpful, for example, if the give-and-take within the family, among friends, and with teachers and mentors is in support of our development—not a give-and-take that diminishes the appetite for further development but one that supports and fuels it.

So, assumption number one is that we want the full embodiment of our inherent possibilities . . . self-realization, to use another term. Critical to this realization is the love and support we receive from others. Also critical is our willingness to do what it takes in order to achieve this realization.

This brings us to assumption number two: Ethical conduct facilitates the fulfillment of inherent possibilities. In one sense, of course, ethical conduct *is* the fulfillment of inherent possibilities. It is one of the ends toward which we are aiming as we develop: the capacity to behave ethically across all situations and settings. But ethical conduct, while an end unto itself, is also a means, requiring us to undo our hardened habits of thinking and doing if those habits hold us back when principle calls us in another direction.

Put another way, through our effort to behave ethically we are brought into contact with the resistances within ourselves with which we must wrestle if we are to unlock and develop our potential as human beings—not just our potential to behave ethically, but our potential (if this is not saying the same thing) to live and work and love creatively.

Thus, through our effort to behave ethically, we acquire self-knowledge. We see the current version of what we are, the person we have made of ourselves; and we see as well the issues we would be wise to address if we are to realize more of our potential.

Before discussing the ethics that move us in the direction of our developmental potential, it is important to discuss what is meant by that phrase. Therefore, a map of life is presented. This map marks the route to our full developmental potential, our inherent possibilities. It also suggests, though implicitly, that it is the attempt to move along this continuum (from the "lower" to the "higher" levels) that marks and helps define the ethical.

THE FIVE LEVELS OF BEING

Figure 1 presents a schematic depicting the five developmental possibilities available to each of us as human beings. These five levels are way stations on what L. Frank Baum in his book *The Wizard of Oz* called the Yellow Brick Road,[4] a metaphor to be used throughout this book. The schematic is a map,[5] or perhaps a poem. It is not science or documented fact. It is an attempt to conjure a feeling for the developmental possibilities available to each of us in the course of a lifetime. It is provided in accord with Schumacher's requirement to show where "the Good is situated."

Read the schematic from left to right, row by row, in order to get a sense of each level as it is defined by the relationship of the descriptors to one another. The levels are arbitrary. They blend into one another and, certainly, there could be more or fewer levels. Even so, there is a direction and a maturation that is mapped.

A brief description of each level follows the presentation of the schematic along with sections that offer an overview of human development (as seen from the vantage point of the schematic).

-- *The Five Levels of Human Development* --

	I	II	III	IV	V
The Five Levels	No Mind →	Hive Mind →	Heroic Mind →	Poetic Mind →	Mature Mind
Group Descriptor	"the innocents"	"the robots"	"the self-actualizers"	"the relativists"	"the free"
What They Mind	infant or damaged genes	what other people think	themselves	their world (their reality)	evolutionary principle
Governing Psychology	approach-avoidance	modeling/ imitation	decision-makers/ goal-oriented operatives	creative role-players	synergetic
Technological Metaphor	"switch"	"mirror"	"thermostat"	"lamp"	"transformer"
What They Seek	satisfaction	acceptance	self-esteem	rhyme & reason	unity/fusion
Level of Biological Organization	cellular	autonomic	somatic	psychosomatic	psychic
Kind of Animal	amoeba	termite/ lemming	eagle	dolphin	human being
Belief Style	prebelievers	believers	disbelievers	suspension of disbelief(ers)	beyond belief
Where They Are Going	nowhere	where the herd takes them	their way	"with the flow"	the stars
Relationship to "System"	system drains	system followers	system rebelers	system makers	system transcenders
What They Harvest	survival	security	territory	vision	soul
Developmental Imperative →	Grow Up! →	Go for It! →	Cultivate the Imagination! →	Turn the Fool Loose!	

Level I: *No Mind*

At Level I is the infant, toddler, or small child, but also the person who is senile or severely mentally disabled. These are the innocents, individuals who are nurtured and furthered along by the family/environment/culture into which they are born or in which they live. We all start out here. Some of us wind up here. Some—through no fault of their own—never leave. Level I is given, a gift by virtue of birth. Each succeeding level, however, must be reached increasingly on our own.

The experience of Level I is driven by need/satisfaction/survival, with consciousness limited to what can be recognized in the moment as nurturing or painful. Oceanic bliss may bathe one moment, while emergency and alarm fill the next. The condition is one of complete dependency. At this level, infants and small children are oriented to the colors, shapes, sounds, tastes, and textures of the world they have so recently entered. Their desires are expressed with cries, spasms, coos, and smiles announcing hunger, discomfort, degree of satisfaction. Against this backdrop, the sense of self is gradually formed as the circuits of trust/distrust are laid and the initial discriminations that relate to survival and wellbeing are learned.

Level I is the opening act, the experience and state of being available to those just entering the play. What happens in subsequent acts (as all students of human development acknowledge) is affected dramatically by what occurs here in this most defenseless and vulnerable of stages. Indeed, one critical measure of a society is the extent to which it cares for those at this level and readies them for further development, neither hampering nor damaging their prospects for maturity or the realization of their potential.[6]

Level II: *Hive Mind*

The focus of Level II is on the socialization of the individual, on developing the individual's capacity to function within society. At Level II, the individual is taught the requirements of fitting into a family, neighborhood, and community. The potential of the developing nervous system is shaped into a thousand specific behaviors allowing conformity, acceptance, and fit. Here the individual is domesticated. The developing self is given a repertoire with which to navigate the demands of the surrounding "hive." Parents, teachers, neighbors, and peers all play a part in the individual's attempt to learn and adapt.

Level II implies that the individual has evolved from absorption in a single point of view (Level I) to an awareness of other points of view. It is a developmental step that brings both complexity and capacity. Through the signs, signals, rewards, and punishments delivered by others and nuanced in increasingly subtle ways, the individual learns what to do and where to go, and also—increasingly—what to think of her own developing abilities. Consciousness includes both social and biological time, as well as an awareness of the acceptance, rejection, and approval/disapproval of others. The individual at Level II understands that there is a hierarchy of roles, a pecking order, and that it is possible to behave both well and badly.

The interior landscape of emotion and feeling is also more complex at Level II. External circumstances or cues sufficiently similar to one another elicit gradations in feeling. To fulfillment and pain are added anticipation, apprehension, anxiety, and fear. To a meaningful degree, the individual has awakened. No longer immersed in the absorption and slumber of Level I, the individual finds himself in training. He is becoming a performer and, in the process, a greater degree of self-awareness becomes possible. The values incorporated into the performance, however, are those of the group, the family/tribe/culture. The individual models those values and, if sufficiently capable, is rewarded (generally) with station and place adequate to his current needs.

The concerns of Levels I and II, respectively, are biological survival and security in the social sphere. They are footing and foundation (Level I) and then platform or stage (Level II) from which to pursue further development. Many, of course, never go beyond Level II. A harsh environment can require the use of all available energy. A harsh culture, community, or family, with punishments that numb the spirit can so disable a person that the thought of further development is hardly a consideration. But if the environment is supportive at all, the intuitive sense of something more remaining intact, then the individual will in time venture forward, proceeding to Level III and perhaps beyond.

Level III: *Heroic Mind*

At Level III, the individual individuates. She separates from the crowd, searching for and attempting to express her own personhood. Perhaps the effort to fit in has proven futile; perhaps rejection or even great good fortune has given rise to a deeper self-examination; perhaps from the individual's earliest days she has been encouraged to go her own way, find her true authentic self; or perhaps (by some mysterious mechanism) there occurs a calculation of the ratio of developmental rate to time yet available and an alarm is triggered. By whatever process, the individual awakens to the need to cut her own course, to make her own distinctive statement, the statement that could not be made in quite the same way were it not for her presence in the world.

And so the individual sets out—heroically, it might be said—to find and express his felt uniqueness. His first steps may be reactionary. He may leave feeling sick of the world with no interest in returning to what he has known. Or he may set out to find the world-saving elixir and, once found, return a hero. But whatever his reason for leaving, he is no longer a believer in things as they are. He now must make his own decisions, set his own goals, show himself and others the power and muscularity of the actualizing self.

Consciousness evolves with each level of development. The tribal/community/hive consciousness of Level II is replaced in Level III with the beginning of an existential consciousness. With choice and uncertainty has come doubt. The individual has awakened to a degree of ambiguity and flux not previously imagined, and to the world's indifference as well. She is on her own, no longer buffered from life's uncertainties by the protections and supports of Level II.

It is here in this newly entered realm that the individual attempts to win a place for himself. He might be successful in his effort—he might indeed win a place for himself—and if so, acquire in the process a self-esteem that fortifies him for further exploration and development. Or he might be unsuccessful in his effort, failing time and again to achieve what he had imagined for himself. But in either case, if the individual remains true to the requirements of Level III—if he continues to pursue his own unique goal(s), not retreating to the mindlessness of previous levels despite the indifference experienced along the way, despite perhaps the many failures—then he is deepened, his understanding of what it takes to survive in this world and to live comfortably within his own skin expanded. He becomes his own person. This and one other thing, not invariably but often: he opens himself to the possibility that the person he has made of himself is incomplete, that there is more to the self-realization project than he had thought. And so, he begins to break with existing patterns, opening himself to the possibility of something beyond what he has achieved through his many efforts at Level III.

Level IV: *Poetic Mind*

With Level IV comes a new degree of objectivity. The individual begins to see through the masks she has been wearing, no longer identifying as strongly with the roles she previously assigned herself. Her developing nonattachment to previous versions of herself is due to a subtle shift in values: As important as where she is going is the process and experience of getting there. She has awakened to her role as director, editor, writer, and producer, seeing her influence over her own experience as never before. What could not be shaped into place heroically is now accepted within a larger context of understanding. As with previous levels, when Level IV is fully experienced, the individual feels she has received a fresh start, a new beginning.

Consciousness at Level IV is marked by a more fully engaged imagination. The individual looks with the mind—consciously so—as much as with the eye. Everywhere, he sees not only what is before him but also, through what is seen, some aspect of himself. He has the detachment to recognize that what he has chosen to see or do, is but one of many, many options; and so, what he has chosen reveals as much about himself and what he values as it does about the world in which he operates. He has achieved a poetic mind, what William Blake called "double vision," and with it a degree of self-awareness and self-understanding not previously enjoyed. The individual now sees how his own history in involved in constructing his experience.

At Level IV, there can occur experiences that seem timeless. The curtain parts if only for a moment, revealing the beauty of all things as they are: the Zen or now-moment that relaxes and renews. The value of these moments is lasting. Whenever they occur (and they can occur at any point along the five level continuum though with greater likelihood here), they can influence the shape and course of a lifetime. For when the curtain closes, the individual realizes—to a degree she could not have realized previously—that she has been too often unconscious (asleep, hypnotized) and, therefore, cut off from an experience of life that is moving and deeply meaningful, an experience that might be available on a far more continuous basis were she to commit herself to realizing further what she now knows is possible.

So, if sufficiently moved by his experience at Level IV, the individual attempts to overcome his "cutoffness."[7] He looks into how he might live more consciously, not wanting his habits of thinking and doing to cause him to miss the experience of his own life. He works to undo even the most subtle aspects of his conditioning so that he can remain present and aware. The individual at Level IV considers that it might be possible to come alive to a degree not previously imagined, and possible, as well, to find greater meaning in the living of his everyday life, and he begins as best he can to explore these possibilities.

Level V: *Mature Mind*[8]

Level V offers the maturity that the individual has sought to some degree all along. With each level, the sense of self has changed, as has the objective or mindset commanding allegiance:

- from a self just beginning to form for which the need for biological survival rules the day (Level I)

- to a self formed through the units of family, community, and local culture, a self that is conscious of other selves and in search of the acceptance and validation that other selves provide (Level II)

- to a self more fully individualized, self-directed, no longer a believer in the party line but a rebel with a cause, a cause that may or may not benefit others but which, at base, is intended to secure a sense of place, worth, and self-esteem (Level III)

- to a self with greater mindfulness, imaginatively engaged, actively working to undermine the hardening habits of thinking and doing that obstruct opportunity, understanding, and the flow of experience (Level IV)

- to a self at the top of its game—integrated, playful, capable of service to the largest of possible motives; a self that through discipline has won its freedom, the freedom to transcend the concerns of all previous levels if duty and service to life so require (Level V)

Throughout this five-level developmental sequence, consciousness has expanded. Increasingly, the individual has become aware of her own conditioning, aware of the subtle ways in which she is perhaps mechanical or robotic, rather than free-flowing and aware. Thus, the individual becomes aware of the importance of undoing or leaving behind the harmful conditioning of the past. Her desire is to operate more often in the present without limits on what she might contribute to it. And yet, to undo or leave behind the unhealthy psychological constraints imposed by past conditioning is an arduous task. Fear can be involved and, with it, motivation for not proceeding, for settling for things as they are. But if the individual does not give up and instead persists, transcending current limits in order to enjoy life and contribute all the more to it, a growing belief in oneself results. Gradually, the individual acquires the ability to be relaxed and at home with herself in a widening circle of people, situations, and settings.

Level V is characterized by the ability to "turn the fool loose," to live unguardedly, playfully, confident that one's intentions are pure, confident also that one can create a peaceful, perhaps loving solution to difficult situations should they arise. Thus, this ability (to turn the fool loose) is an achievement of a very high order. It is a moral or ethical achievement. Only after the individual has rid himself of his self-destructiveness as well as his need to create interpersonal tension in order to feel defined[9] is it safe for him to freely share what he has made of himself. At Level V, the individual realizes that of all the gifts he might give others, the gift that is certain to be a contribution is his embodiment of a fully mature self, creatively and ethically involved with the possibilities of the moment. Respect for the best in others is expressed in this way, as is one's love of life. The individual who achieves this level of conduct on a consistent basis is a moral force, a part in conscious service to the whole. By his behavior, such an individual continues to further his own development while also stirring awareness and encouraging psychic integration in others.

Consider again the course the individual has traveled to reach Level V. With each developmental step, the individual's capacity to integrate information to the benefit of self and other has increased. As this has happened, the individual has relaxed, allowing still more information to enter. The valves that govern inflow are open wide, and though they can (and should) be closed as required, the energy to activate every receptor increasingly passes through them. The individual feels alive and connected as never before, and with this aliveness comes a willingness to aid others (life itself) in their unfolding. And to the extent that she does aid others (in whatever way is right for her), the individual feels as though she is fulfilling at least some part of her purpose, no longer cut off to the same degree from herself or from what matters. To return to the schematic, the individual at Level V is not solely amoeba, lemming, eagle, or dolphin, however sturdy, noble, or inspiring these forms of existence may be. She is now a psychologically and spiritually mature human being, perhaps the rarest of evolution's flowers and perhaps, as well, the most instrumental to its cause.

THE NATURE OF DEVELOPMENT

So, for the purposes of this book, these five levels divide and mark the continuum of human possibility, forming a map of the developmental levels available to each of us as we travel the Yellow Brick Road. And lest this map appear too simplistic, and therefore unlike life as we know it, it should be noted that development is rarely steady, and never certain. It would be unusual for an adult to be solidly or completely at only one level. Most of us are all over this five-level continuum.

Consider, for example, the variation in personal relationships: In some relationships, we find we operate predominately from Level II, expressing the values and views of the other person, living their program and their prescription, their approval and acceptance vital to us for whatever reason. In other relationships, we may operate predominately from Level III, interacting and exchanging with others so as to further our goals, perceiving and treating others as a means to our ends. And in still other relationships, perhaps, we are able to operate predominately from Level V, with love and regard for what is best for us and the other person over the long run.

The same sort of variation can be observed across differing situations. In some situations, we are ill at ease, dependent, waiting for others to define our experience, operating from Level I and feeling deeply uncomfortable. At other times, we are confident, at ease with ourselves, able to interact creatively with what is before us (Levels IV/V).

Only on average are we located at a specific developmental level.[10] With specific people in specific situations at specific times, we may operate above our average, rising to the occasion and enjoying ourselves in the process. At other times, we may behave below our average, lacking the energy and vision to come up to the level where we currently live our lives from day to day. The individual at Level II has moments of pure poetry, moments that transcend Level II development, just as he has moments governed by feelings of complete dependency—but these moments are rare, not the rule. On balance, he lives at Level II, modeling the behavior of others and seeking security in their acceptance.

The fundamental edict—the developmental imperative—regardless of where one is situated on average, however, is to engage the present moment so as to further the development of self and other. In that way, the meaning of present experience is enhanced and progress on the Yellow Brick Road ensured. With that progress comes the ability to bring advantage to those we care about and to ourselves. As indicated previously, we want that advantage—the fulfillment of inherent possibilities. Though there is invariably great difficulty in reaching the higher developmental levels, the motivation to do so runs deep. It springs, simply, from self-interest, the desire to find what supports and enhances not only survival but also quality of life, and to avoid what does not. And this implies, among many other things, a growing capacity to utilize and manage the potentialities of the self, including, of course, the potentialities of the self with others.

Thus, we travel the Yellow Brick Road for reasons of self-interest. It is true that our appetite for proceeding may be dampened along the way, even distorted, as discussed in the next section. Still, the path lies in one direction and, so, the Good to which Schumacher referred.

DEVELOPMENTAL DISORDER

What keeps us from smooth, continuous development? Perhaps it would be better to ask what retards our development, giving us sustained periods of no growth at all. It is, for want of a better term, the disorder we fall into along the way. With every step and at any moment, it is possible for things to go awry.

Consider, for example, the abused child. Developmental trajectory is established in the early years of life. With nurturing and care, this trajectory is optimized, the child made ready for the requirements of Level II and beyond. With abuse, however, or neglect of whatever sort, the trajectory can be inhibited, perhaps in ways that remain undetected for years. The individual may discover later in life a lack of readiness for the increasingly subtle requirements of adulthood. It is of course possible to repair this damage, to put right the trajectory, but not without difficulty. The discipline and commitment that is required of the individual, and the art, acceptance, and unconditional love that are so helpful to the repair process, are not altogether common. Without these ingredients, however, the distortions imposed by childhood abuse can exert their influence for a lifetime. This is what the French philosopher Sartre was suggesting when he said, "Childhood decides";[11] not the whole truth, by any means, but a chilling sentence given the truth it does contain.

Similarly, at any point in life there can occur abuse, trauma, or loss of a magnitude beyond what we are capable of withstanding, bringing a confusion or disorder so severe that further development is brought to a halt. Depression of the severest sort can follow, the loss of what was once a hearty appetite for life. To the individual in this state, the entire notion that there might be some level of integration at which point the pain is healed and perspective restored seems like a lie the as-yet-unaffected tell themselves.

There is also a compounding effect that can come from our effort to escape the pain associated with the disorder in our lives. Instead of dealing directly with the disorder, we turn to whatever will offer relief. This is understandable and may work for a time, but increasingly, in our effort to find relief, we must increase the dose of whatever provides relief. Opiates, shopping, sex, television, prescription medications, alcohol, even our work can offer escape and, thus, relief—at least for a while. But in time, if engaged in often enough, each of these escapes can create an appetite that if not fed, results in withdrawal cravings. We can find ourselves engaging in our chosen escape not so much for the pleasure or relief it affords but because by engaging in it, we avoid the anxiety now associated with its absence. This is addiction, the route by which we add disorder to our life while the disorder we were attempting to escape remains unaddressed.

Disorder and disorientation, whatever their source (trauma, abuse, loss, etc.) and however they might be compounded (addiction), must be addressed in order for development to proceed. Indeed, addressing disorder is one of the ways in which development occurs, and one of the ways in which we can create readiness for further growth. To address our disorder (or to help others address theirs), whatever form the disorder takes, is to engage in ethical behavior. It is such improvements—whether in oneself or in the culture—that make self-and other-destructiveness less likely and progress on the Yellow Brick Road, evolution itself, more likely. This is one of the themes that runs throughout the ethics of human development and, in particular, in what is called the Personal Growth Ethic: *Namely, it is ethical to address the developmental requirements of the self, unethical not to do so; ethical to increase the capacity for ethical conduct in self and others, unethical to stop growing as a person—this so that a greater, more inclusive order can evolve, creatively, consciously, with less violence and harm to self and others in the process.*

THE FUNDAMENTAL IGNORANCE

Two things, should they occur, are helpful for the realization of inherent possibilities. Development can occur without them, but with far less certainty. Both have to do with the culture in which we find ourselves.

First, it is helpful if the culture into which our development has taken us is welcoming, responding as though it recognizes us and is delighted we have arrived. When this happens, we feel seen, heard, and valued (e.g., the gifted elementary school teacher who acknowledges and celebrates the presence of each child on the first day of school, or the mother who, ready for parenthood, welcomes, nurtures, and embraces the newborn child). Second, it is helpful if that same culture labors to render us free of the need to be recognized and, so, able to withstand the indifference of the larger culture if the dictates of our development require it.

Welcoming is crucial. Without it, we may lack the sense of safety and assuredness needed for integration and learning. At the same time, the promotion of the independence that allows us to continue to integrate and learn in the absence of support is also crucial. Without that, we can be stifled, made dependent and, eventually, unable to move beyond the limits of current cultural and institutional practice, beyond current worldviews. We will lack the strength to explore our inherent possibilities and perhaps—by our efforts—bring new possibilities within range for others.

To put it another way, society, culture, its institutions—whether family, school, or workplace—serve the individual (and ultimately themselves) to the extent that they respect the individual by rendering him independent, self-reliant, his own person. And they do this in part by welcoming, honoring, and treating as inviolate the individual's uniqueness. They must teach him what they know (if they can), hone and refine his capacities in a thousand directions. But in doing so, they must also aid and support the emergence of his independence. In this way, an individual emerges, a person, with a growing justification for believing in his own capacity to meet the future, whatever it might hold.

At some point, perhaps as the individual is learning to think for herself, it is also helpful to inform her of what is believed to be her potential as a human being, her inherent possibilities, and to do so thoughtfully, with openness and care—letting her know about the Yellow Brick Road (in whatever terms are appropriate), its stages or levels of being, and about her right to realize this potential if she can cultivate and practice the discipline it requires. When depression or what is sometimes called the great doubt enters her life, as is likely in the course of a lifetime, she will have this understanding, gathered from trusted elders, to fall back on.

It is not an exaggeration to suggest that the majority of humankind has no idea of the possibilities residing within the self. The institutions of far too many cultures have failed to serve the larger, long-term cause of human development. As a consequence, far too many of us, in the midst of our everyday lives, conclude that we have found all in the way of wellbeing that is available to us. It is a tragedy, a kind of darkness over the land, for without a knowledge of our developmental/inherent possibilities, without the effort to convey this knowledge to all individuals as they set out on their life journey, without an understanding of the Yellow Brick Road and where it leads, we ensure greater alienation and loss than need occur. We serve not evolution or awareness or human development, but entropy. And why? Are we ignorant of the waste and despair that ignorance itself brings? Only by informing those on the path (and all of us are potentially on the path) of the developmental possibilities residing within the self—and readying them, as just discussed, to travel it—do we counter the ignorance and cynicism that accompanies the loss of hope. "The deepest ignorance is not to know about the window,"[12] said Rumi, the thirteenth-century poet, by which he may have meant (at least in part) being unaware of or unable to see through to the profound possibilities of the self; not to know that beyond the confines of walled-in experience—the hardened habits governing our lives and with which we see the world—more exists in the way of personal discovery and psychological growth.

WORK AS METAPHOR

It might be clarifying at this point to depart from the general overview and focus for a moment on the world of work and, in particular, on how the pursuit of mastery in a chosen profession can mirror the larger journey we are on as individuals.

Consider, for example, the architect:

No Mind. The would-be architect starts out a neophyte, an innocent, ignorant of the terms, concepts, and skills required in order to function effectively in his craft. He starts out with the basics and approaches them with some trepidation, concerned that he might not be able to make them his own.

Hive Mind. As he proceeds, through classes or an internship, he learns the basics and applies them in accord with the rules and practices of the profession. He functions as a true believer, seeking the acceptance and sanction of his chosen profession, winning his certificate to practice his place in the guild.

Heroic Mind. At some point, the now-certified architect desires more; the anonymity of being simply another member of the guild, of blindly following its prescriptions to the resolution of the same problems time and again, is stifling, and he rebels. He now feels he must see more of himself in what he is doing. He must test himself on new problems, new issues, perhaps make a name for himself, contribute to the field by moving beyond his (or perhaps its) current boundaries.

Poetic Mind. Eventually, however, the task of making a name for himself (if that is his aim) or of moving beyond current practices to new territory must be tempered; it must have an aesthetic edge. The work he is doing must catch the eye and appeal to a more refined sensibility; it must have elegance. For this reason, a poetic sensibility is cultivated and brought into the work. Projects must delight or challenge, as they are not simply bridges or buildings or earthworks but statements with a rhyme or reason embedded in them, capable of expanding the viewer (just as they have expanded the architect) if the viewer has the capacity to see what is there.

Mature Mind. Finally, with persistence (and certainly not on every occasion), the architect is able to transcend all prescriptions, all requirements, and thus to work without the pull of ego, school of thought, or romantic/poetic consideration. Here is creative freedom, the opportunity to bring to bear the capacities acquired and exercised in all previous levels without the need to impose any of them, only the need to meet fully—with the fullest set of considerations in mind—the requirements of the task at hand. Here is conscious, meaningful absorption in one's work, what one produces, and how one goes about it, presenting and embodying the ideal.

This way of viewing the route to mastery can be applied to any art, profession, skill, or sport. And though by this view the process is simplified—learning involves oscillation, contact with error as well as with success—still, it is possible to look past the complexity, past also the the years devoted to a given endeavor, and see reflected the Yellow Brick Road. Consider the downhill skier. Here the terms are different than those used with the architect, as is the tone, but the route to mastery is nonetheless mapped by the same five levels.

No Mind: In the beginning, the would-be skier says, "I'm going to try not to fall; that's my goal. I just don't want to break anything." And in so saying, the student adopts an amoeboid, survival-based, approach-avoidance attitude toward the sport.

Hive Mind: As the student improves, the attitude changes. The student says, "I'm going to do exactly as the instructor prescribes. I'm going to stay right in her tracks, modeling and mirroring her every move." And so, the student embraces the experience programmed by authority.

Heroic Mind: As the skill of the student increases, she sooner or later leaves her instructor. She abandons the restrictiveness of the class experience for the sake of the self. "I can make my own way down the mountain," she says. "I'll meet the rest of you at the lift!"

Poetic Mind: With increasing success and diminishing fulfillment, the student awakens to the flow. "Wait a minute," she says. "It's how I go down the mountain that really matters. I'm going to put so much rhyme and reason into this descent that they will have to peal the smile off my face!" The student becomes an acrobat, a downhill racer, a dolphin diving and returning to the surface.

Mature Mind: At last, tired of her play, the student remembers her desire only to feel unlimited, and so in a certain sense gives up thinking altogether, submitting herself fully to the factors of snow, slope, wind, and x-squared. It is as if she says, "The mountain does the thinking, and I ski its line of thought." It's at that point that she becomes the master of her own descent.

The point is that mastery of a profession, art, or discipline can be viewed as being obtained by the same course traveled to reach mastery of the self. With this realization, we are able to see and be reminded of the path we are on as individuals, reminded that we are—when it comes to the self—a work in progress, pursuing whatever mastery or enlightenment is ours to obtain. Seeing the five levels mirrored in our professional life, in our moments of pure mastery (if we have them), allows us to see more clearly what is required to develop the self. We have a marker, a touch of what it is like to engage and serve fully and skillfully a single moment, however extended, without distractedness, preoccupation, or unneeded self-protectiveness. We see what it takes (or part of what it takes), because in this one area of life we have tasted it: the very best of ourselves in situations that matter, a transcendence past the superfluous, past the self-conscious, to a creative and honoring matchup with the task at hand. Other areas of our life may be a mess, but here, in our profession (or art or discipline), we have given the time and focus needed to reap, on occasion, a realization of true mastery. And in moments of reflection, whether architect, skier, or short-order cook, we see that our accomplishment is but a metaphor, a reminder of what we must do with the self, a reminder of the journey we are on to a more integrated, wholesome mode of being in which a more complete range of interpersonal requirements are met with effectiveness and grace—not as an expert in every area of life, but as a self-mastered individual, a life artist perhaps, with, among other things, the ability to share rather than obstruct the best that is in us.[13]

EVOLUTION'S RAREST FLOWER

It is a rare individual who achieves her full maturity, who is stably situated at Level V. But one of the many things that characterize the conduct of such an individual—or that characterizes Level V conduct whenever we engage in it, though we might not engage in it consistently—is the honoring of all levels in the developmental sequence.[14] That is what characterizes the mature individual: His or her conduct reflects an allegiance to human development overall and, thus, to an honoring of each level as a part of a process that, if not stifled or in some way distorted, serves the expansion of awareness and the flourishing of life as a whole. Prior to Level V, our motives are less expansive and certainly less conscious.

At Level I, for example, the individual is driven instinctively by concerns for survival (and necessarily so). At Level II, the focus is on security and acceptance, on readying the individual for membership in family/community/society. Level III champions the right of the individual to stand out, to strengthen the position of the self within existing contexts, and to win and/or acquire territory (of whatever sort), while Level IV addresses the need for rhyme and reason, the need to experience these conditions, to see and create with them in mind. Only with Level V do we integrate all previous motives into a larger framework that recognizes the value of each without allowing any one to be preeminent. Each is seen and honored as a developmental step readying the individual with the capacity to embrace the next step without allowing any step to serve as an end point. Indeed, from the vantage point of Level V, there is no end point, though a critical point is reached when development itself is valued and made the focus.[15]

In the end, of course, it is behavior—choices and the values revealed by those choices—that defines our level of development. The behavior of those at Level V is characterized by the artful inviting out of human potential, the skillful shepherding and shaping of progress on the Yellow Brick Road (though not by shaping and interaction alone but also by example and inspiration). Behavior of this sort, with ends so clearly in service to others, can penetrate defenses (not invariably but with greater likelihood than any other means) and be recognized as friendly to our deepest and most essential nature. It is true that individuals who exhibit conduct of this sort can unintentionally threaten others with their freedom, their capacity to disregard the conventions that hold others of us in place. Still, the reason in and for their behavior, if glimpsed at all, is disarming. It is natural to be taken with what they model: the freedom to be natural,[16] the fool turned loose with no ill intent left in him, the playfulness and compassion that spring from the person in love with life. We are drawn to them because they model the realization of our desire to be liberated and whole. They speak to the best that is in us and to what we would have more of if we can find our way to it: enlightenment, adulthood in the fullest sense, realizing that it flowers differently in every individual who achieves it. We can thwart the pull exerted by their example. We can be deeply suspicious of levels of development different from our own. And, for whatever reason, most of us do step off the path long before we reach Level V adulthood. Still, the desire for the realization of inherent possibilities remains. Our heads are turned by the beauty we see in others—the behavioral or ethical beauty, and we reach for it, at some level identifying with it, even if we are unable to exhibit it ourselves.

SUMMARY

The opening passage of Part I quoted economist E. F. Schumacher: "If a thing is said to be good but no one can tell me what it is good for, how can I be expected to take any interest in it? If our guide, our annotated Map of Life, cannot show us where The Good is situated and how it can be reached, it is worthless." Part I has been an attempt to address the first part of Schumacher's concern: to show by means of a map of life where the Good is situated. It lies, according to the map presented here, in the direction of our development as integrated, free, and enlightened selves, creatively and ethically engaged in furthering that same development in others. In that direction (and in that development) lies leverage on the present. Increasingly, both our capacity and our inclination to make choices that further human development—that further the human experiment, itself—are enhanced, making more likely a peaceful, creative, and ethical future.

As to the second part of Schumacher's concern ("How can The Good be reached?"), Part II discusses the ethics of human development.

Part II

Human Logic and the Ethics of Human Development

> "The outstanding character of the hyper-organic level (of evolution) is the emergence of selves . . . It is the development or realization of selves that constitutes the 'good' . . . and the theory of ethics that makes this the locus of value is called the ethics of self-realization. By this is meant that the locus of the good is not found in pleasure, nor in organic survival or welfare, but in the complete energizing of our capacities as selves or persons."[1]
>
> —Wilbur Marshall Urban
> *Fundamentals of Ethics*

Ethics, as the term is used in this book, is defined as human logic,[2] the logic by which we are made human. Or, to soften the definition slightly, ethics as human logic means the code of conduct or behavioral rules by which we educate, mature, and enlighten ourselves.

This definition has several implications for the discussion that follows, but chief among them is the notion that neither by birth nor by the passage of time is the full human maturity described in Part I ensured. Rather, that degree of maturity is best thought of as an achievement, something obtained through conscious and deliberate effort.

The ethics presented in Part II are an attempt to give body and detail to the notion of human logic. Called the ethics of human development, they aim us in a direction that energizes our capacities as selves or persons. Before discussing these ethics, two points are worth making. First, it is no doubt true that we can be educated, matured, perhaps even enlightened by any number of means. Even the most wasteful and destructive ways of living—to take the extreme—can result in a turnaround; we do, on occasion, wake up by banging our heads against the wall (figuratively speaking). But what we wake up to, if we do wake up, is to the cost of living unconsciously, the cost of not thinking before we act. Though we may not express it this way, we wake up to the value of living consciously, of interrupting unconscious patterns of behavior with forethought, for example, or of simply behaving with more awareness in general. It is possible to be educated, matured, perhaps even enlightened by other means, but the ethics of human development are an attempt to help us cut a more direct route to those desired ends and, in the process, minimize the harm we otherwise might do to ourselves and others along the way.

The second point—perhaps a corollary of the first—is this: We are creatures of habit. We have established patterns of behavior. The prospect of venturing beyond our established patterns can be daunting given the inertia likely to be involved. At the same time, countering this inertia is our desire to experience and demonstrate our highest potential as human beings, to find and express the best that is in us and to make with our lives a beneficial difference. However obscure this desire or however distracted from it we are, it is there according to the assumption offered in Part I, calling on us to explore the higher reaches of our own development. To behave in accord with the ethics of human development, and to do so consistently, is challenging. But it is by such behavior—as well as by other means—that we serve our desire for further development while also strengthening the social and biological environments on which we depend.

THE ETHICS OF HUMAN DEVELOPMENT

The ethics of human development could be called the ethics of personal responsibility, the ethics of right livelihood, the ethics of personal growth, the ethics of teamwork and collaboration, or even, to borrow Wilbur Marshall Urban's phrase, the ethics of self-realization. In the training program on which much of this book is based, they were called the ethics of choice. By whatever name, they are an attempt to establish a behavioral ideal. Terms like *trust*, *integrity*, *fairness*, *respect*—terms so often found in ethical codes—are, for the most part, not found in this code because here, the attempt is to detail how one *operates* when behaving with these qualities. Here, the attempt is to leave behind the looseness of these terms and in the process, hopefully, invite a greater degree of clarity, as well as a greater degree of self-examination.

At the same time, a qualification to this "ideal" is required. The ethics of human development offer a prescription, a recipe—one that aims us in the direction of what is most likely the proper course of action. Still, there are exceptions. Some situations may call for behavior other than the behavior prescribed by the code. In those cases, our allegiance must be to the moment, the situation at hand, and not to the code. The expert chef follows the recipe to a T unless knowledge or intuition tells her that by varying the recipe, she can create a more perfect dish. The ethics presented here point us in the direction most likely to serve the cause of human development, but may not always serve that cause depending on the variables at play. They prescribe the best direction in which to err if in doubt.

It is worth pointing out, however, that our ability to discern and make legitimate exceptions to the code improves with advancing development. Too often, we make exceptions not because the situation calls for it but because we are afraid to proceed. As development advances, fear less often rules the day, and the honoring of oneself and others, regardless of fear or momentary difficulty, increasingly wins out (this being one measure of personal development).

So, to reiterate, the ethics of human development are an attempt to give body and detail to the notion of human logic, to operationalize the concept. The aim and fundamental value is human development, one's own and that of others. And while many variables come into play in any given situation (gender, race, class, ethnicity, etc.)—variables that may call for exceptions and/or differences in style or expression—the attempt with this code is to reach past those differences to the humanity we have in common.

What follows are the twelve ethics of human development. The first to be considered is the Organizational Ethic, the ethic that focuses most specifically on our life in organizations, primarily the workplace. To this ethic, the others are added, never leaving the workplace or organizations in general but gradually expanding the sense of what is meant by organization to encompass society as a whole and, so, the full range of everyday life.

"Here, in this poor, hampered, despicable Actual, wherein even now thou standest, here or nowhere is thy Ideal: work it out Therefrom."

Zeno
Quoted in *Marcus Aurelius*
—Henry Dwight Sedgwick

". . . This is the final meaning of work: the extension of human consciousness."

—D. H. Lawrence
English Novelist and Poet

Ethic 1

The Organizational Ethic

It is ethical to serve, refine, and advance the organization you have chosen to join. It is unethical to harm it.

If we feel we have chosen for ourselves the organization of which we are a part, that we have come to it voluntarily and, thus, that it is worthy of our involvement, then our task is to serve it, refine it, advance it to the best of our ability. Our task is to help it find and realize its potential. In so doing, we discover that we must find, express, and perhaps expand our own potential. We must, for example, acquire new skills, refine and practice existing skills, overcome our disinclination to do either, assume responsibility for outcomes, manage our energy level and our attitude. Thus, by this ethic we serve the development of both organization and self. Each is advanced by our effort.

On the other hand, to harm the organization, its prospects for survival and long-term success, is to harm ourselves, since our success—other things being equal—is bound up with the success of the organization.

Beyond that, however, should the organization not succeed despite our best efforts to serve it, then we will have benefited nevertheless since by our efforts we will have kept our capacity to contribute exercised. We will have kept ourselves ready and in practice should we choose to join another organization. So, in more than one way, we harm ourselves by not attempting to serve, refine, and advance the organization of which we are a part. On the one hand, our prospects for success, wrapped up as they are with the success of the organization, diminish as the organization falters and, on the other hand, our capacity to serve and contribute weakens as we fail to exercise it.

There are ten corollaries that accompany Ethic 1. Together they help define what it means to serve, refine, and advance the organization we have chosen to join.

Corollary 1:
It is ethical to learn everything you can about the organization of which you are a part, including its overall purpose; the vision that guides it; its rules, practices, and procedures; its parts and how they are connected; its history and current status. It is unethical to remain organizationally ignorant.

The more we know about the organization of which we are a part (i.e., its strengths and weaknesses, the direction in which it wishes to grow, etc.), the more likely we are to know its needs. This puts us in a position to help it, to innovate to its advantage.

Further, the more we know about the organization, the less likely we are to undermine it unknowingly, i.e., the less likely we are to make changes in one part of the organization that have undesired consequences in other parts of the organization. In other words, the more we know about the organization, the more able we are to consider the whole when deciding to act in any one section or part.

Finally, the more we know about the organization (what it stands for, what it is seeking to accomplish, etc.), the more likely we are to recognize offers, proposals, and courses of action that represent conflicts of interest. The sooner a potential conflict of interest is detected, the easier it is to avoid or correct. This helps to spare all involved from problems that can have serious legal, ethical, and financial implications.

All this being said, we obviously cannot know everything about the organization(s) of which we are a part. There is often too much complexity. But we can continue to learn, discover, and deepen our knowledge, with particular focus on the organization's goals, practices, and products. The spirit of Corollary 1 is this: Learn everything you can about your organization and continue to learn—with special emphasis on the essentials—lest you wake up later in life to the realization that you have been serving something you do not believe in. For your own well-being, it is important that you serve an organization whose purpose and means are acceptable to you, whose ethics and values are consistent with your own. It is important that you feel your life being well used through affiliations established because you believe in them. It is dishonoring to yourself and to those with whom you are involved to do otherwise.

Corollary 2:
It is ethical to learn about the needs of those served by your organization (i.e., who they are and what they value), and it is also ethical to learn about the needs of those within the organization who are served by your division or part. It is unethical to remain ignorant of the needs of those you serve, whether they are customers, consumers, clients, students, or fellow employees.

Ultimately, the survival of any organization depends on its ability to meet the needs of those it serves. If their needs are not met, they will go elsewhere, dropping their affiliation and no longer contributing their resources—in whatever form—to the organization. An organization cannot sustain itself without the support of those it exists to serve.

Of course, the degree to which an organization can meet the needs of those it serves depends to a considerable extent on the degree to which individuals within the organization meet the work and performance needs of one another. Thus, each member of the organization must strive to meet the work needs of internal consumers/customers/workmates/etc. By meeting those needs, internal kinks are removed and organizational performance improves.

Thus, the more we know about those we serve, whether inside or outside the organization, the more productively creative we can be. Our knowledge of their needs puts us in a position to refine existing products, practices, and procedures, and to invent new ones. This increases the organization's value to those it serves and so, its likelihood of survival and success.

Behind this corollary, however, is the notion discussed briefly in the preface: We serve ourselves when we serve others (i.e., the gift is to the giver). By serving others effectively, whether they are inside or outside the organization, we not only increase our value to them and to the organization as a whole but we also feel the satisfaction that comes from service to others. Other things being equal, we more readily can conclude that our time and energy are being well spent.

Corollary 3:
It is ethical to perform your role (i.e., your job or duty) accurately, efficiently, and pleasantly. It is unethical not to do your job to the best of your ability.

Inaccuracy, inefficiency, and rudeness all mean more errors in performance and, thus, greater variation in the quality of the products and services an organization is able to provide. This variation and decline in quality threatens organizational success. Add to this the fact that where inaccuracy, inefficiency, and rudeness go unchecked, stress and frustration mount. As a consequence, the organization becomes a less appealing place for both its members/employees and its customers/consumers.

Take but one example: the individual who keeps work away by bristling whenever approached. Others, including managers and supervisors, may begin to avoid this individual since they experience only trouble when they interact with him. This avoidance builds inefficiencies into the organization, as well as resentments as others in the organization find they must carry more than their fair share or as they notice others catching the same distasteful manner. Rudeness and unpleasantness undermine organizational effectiveness (see Corollary 4).

It is important to note that organizations hire us or otherwise invite us to join in order to do a job or fulfill a role. The expectation is that the job will be performed to the best of our ability (i.e., among other things, accurately, efficiently, and pleasantly). To fail to do so is to compromise the performance of the organization and, beyond that, to break the trust, violating the expectation of a fair exchange.

Further, it is only by performing to the best of our ability that we can know or expand our ability. To go through the motions, to coast or phone in our performance, is to allow our ability to deteriorate and our muscles to atrophy. Our best will not be available when we need it, a fact that we, as well as others, will notice. The result, though perhaps gradual, is a loss of self-esteem as we witness our willingness to settle for less than we are capable of giving.

Corollary 4:
It is ethical to perform your role (i.e., your job or duty) in a fashion that does not add to the work, hardship, or distraction of others unnecessarily. It is unethical to make work unnecessarily harder for others.

The more unnecessary work, hardship, and/or distraction we impose on others, the more difficult we make their situation, making it all the harder for them to perform in an accurate, efficient, and pleasant manner. The result is that errors increase, quality varies, and the organization as a whole experiences the slowdown that comes from resentment, drift, and stress-related burnout.

According to those who have been in prison, one rule predominates: Do your own time! To do someone else's time (i.e., to make it harder for them to do their time by adding unnecessary work, hardship, or distraction) is to invite repercussions, sometimes of a rather serious sort. It is the same in all organizations. To do someone else's time by adding unnecessary work, hardship, or distraction is to invite resentment and create resistance. The result is a loss of interpersonal effectiveness and, eventually, an increase in interpersonal tension.

At the same time, it is true that we can sometimes be confused about what is and is not necessary, what is and is not appropriate. What we believe is unnecessary may in fact be necessary. This is something we would know if we saw fully how the pieces of the organization fit together. Therefore, it is important to seek from others an understanding of how current tasks and requests fit in, and equally important when making requests of others to relate those requests to legitimate organizational ends. By these practices, organizational awareness expands (Corollary 1), as does our skill at both informing and remaining informed.

This corollary further invites us to consider how our neediness or lack of self-awareness can result in an inadvertent, perhaps unconscious, spilling over on to others. Desiring escape from boredom, stress, or anxiety, we find that we seek rescue from others, only to discover (or to be told, or perhaps never be told) that there is or may be an inconsiderateness or selfishness or lack of regard for others in our behavior—that we are allowing our needs to blind us to the needs of others, or to the needs of the organization. That's not to say that the needs we are attempting to address are not legitimate. They no doubt are legitimate. But our decision to address them as we are may be counterproductive, creating hidden costs for both ourselves and the organization.

It's also the case that we may simply be ignorant of the etiquette or manners appropriate to a particular culture of work or play. We may be ignorant of the many ways we can find ourselves walking across the green while others are attempting to putt. Through our lack of awareness, then, or our lack of self-control once we become aware, we may cause hardship, distraction, and/or unnecessary work for others. The result is that things become harder, not easier. More energy is required to accomplish the same or less, instead of the other way around. In the end, whether by ignorance or lack of discipline, organizational capacity is reduced.

So, with this corollary, as with many of the others, the underlying theme is: Expand awareness and with that expanded and expanding awareness exert control over your conduct so that you are not unconsciously thwarting your own effectiveness or the effectiveness of others.

Corollary 5:
It is ethical to speak fairly and honestly of organizational members; to say *about* them what you are willing to say *to* them. The same applies to the organization as a whole. It is unethical to engage in malicious gossip, ridicule, or derisive humor.

Nothing so creates disharmony within an organization as do critical comments made about, but not *to*, the parties in question. The actions that flow from these comments—particularly comments grounded in prejudice, anger, or fear—can be extremely destructive not only to those being discussed but to the organization itself. For an individual to discover that he or she is the subject of malicious gossip, ridicule, or derisive humor is for that individual to feel dishonored. It is enough to break the trust necessary for organizational effectiveness. And when trust is broken in this way, it is slow to return.

Further, to say *about* others what we will not say *to* them dishonors not only the parties spoken of but also ourselves. At some level, we know or come to know that we are allowing fear, resentment, and/or anger to direct us rather than duty or principle. Instead of seizing our opportunity for personal growth by saying what must be said to the party in question or deciding that it need not be said at all, we fall back into avoidance or denial. We seek individuals with whom to confirm our prejudices rather than choosing to help others, ourselves, and/or the organization evolve.

To be clear, this corollary is not about gossip per se, nor about relating informal news within a network of friends and associates. It is about malicious gossip, ill intent. It is not about good-natured teasing or playfulness. It is about ridicule. And it is not about the absence of humor or taking away the opportunity to bond with others through humor. It is about derisiveness, about making others (who would not find it funny) the butt of the joke. In the end, it is about examining our motives and adjusting our speech until they are self-honoring and consistent with the requirements of a culture marked by trust, directness, and candor.

Corollary 6:
It is ethical to follow the rules, practices, and procedures of the organization. It is unethical to willfully and knowingly violate the rules, practices, and procedures of the organization or to remain ignorant of them.

At the same time, it is naive to think that rules are never to be broken. Therefore, it is ethical to make exceptions to rules, practices, and procedures when such exceptions serve or do not harm the organization. Further, it is ethical to share the reasoning behind these exceptions so that this reasoning can be examined and refined and so that others in the organization can sooner recognize when and where exceptions are appropriate. It is ethical to help others in the organization acquire the discernment that allows them to make exceptions to rules, practices, and procedures when such exceptions serve or do not harm the organization.

The rules, practices, and procedures of the organization exist because it is believed or, perhaps, has been found that conduct in accord with them maximizes organizational effectiveness. To willfully and knowingly break the rules, practices, or procedures, or to disregard them by remaining ignorant of them, is to diminish organizational effectiveness and, in the end, to threaten organizational survival.

When the prescribed rules of an organization are violated and such violations remain a secret (as they often do, at least for a while), then it is impossible to factor such violations into the ongoing effort to account for variations in organizational performance. Performance variations due to these violations wind up being attributed to other factors. The organization's lack of awareness concerning what is really causing the issue hinders its ability to take corrective action and so hinders its ability to develop and evolve. Or, to put it differently, only by following the prescribed rules of the organization can we judge their adequacy and whether or not they effectively steer energy and resources in accord with the organization's espoused mission. Based on what we discover, we can then make needed revisions and improvements (Corollaries 7 and 8).

Further, to break the rules that we agreed to follow when joining the organization is to break the trust. When this is discovered, organizations respond by adding new layers of policing to ensure compliance. Thus, those who willfully and knowingly break the rules without attempting to correct them (as in Corollary 7) wind up making the organization more restrictive and so, for many, a less desirable place to be.

That is not to say, however, that rules are never to be broken. As this corollary points out, there are times when breaking a rule either serves or does not harm the organization. Although the established rules of the organization prescribe the most desirable way to proceed, there will be exceptions. However, when these exceptions occur, it is ethical to share the reasoning behind them so that this reasoning can be examined, refined, and perhaps even sanctioned. This permits others in the organization to learn when and under what circumstances exceptions may be appropriate.

Finally, the organization's rules etc. reflect, in operational terms, its aspirations for itself—how it believes it should function in the world. By adhering to these rules, we give ourselves the opportunity to see whether the organization is an acceptable, appropriate, even worthy day-to-day fit for us. If it is a good fit, we eliminate by degree the dividedness, if any, we feel about being a part of it. If not, we put before ourselves, sooner rather than later, critical questions concerning our affiliation and whether or not we can have an effect, make a difference, or simply be comfortable with ourselves while we are a part of the organization.

> **Corollary 7:**
> **It is ethical to seek the correction, modification, and/or revision of rules, practices, and procedures that are inconsistent with the overall purpose and stated values of the organization. It is unethical to accept without seeking to correct organizational practices that harm the ability of the organization to accomplish its purpose.**

Corollary 6 requires Corollary 7; they are companion corollaries. For not only are there rules, practices, and procedures to which, on occasion, exceptions can be made (Corollary 6), but there are sometimes rules, practices and procedures that are no longer consistent with the mission and stated values of the organization. To go along with such practices without seeking to correct them is to ignore our responsibility both to the organization and to ourselves. Rules that do not serve the organization are a waste of time. To allow them to remain is to diminish organizational effectiveness.

Of course, it is possible to be wrong about a rule needing to be changed or a practice needing to be altered (a statement that foreshadows Ethic 2). While we may be convinced of the need for a change in this or that rule or practice, others in the organization may disagree and may vote or otherwise decide to keep things as they are. Further, because of our exchange with them, we may come to agree, discovering that our view was incomplete and that good reasons exist for leaving the rule or practice unchanged. Or we may remain convinced: The rule or practice is at odds with the best interests of the organization despite what others say. If that is our view then we are left with a dilemma. Can we accept the compromise imposed by leaving the rule or practice in place? Can we continue to give our full support to the organization? Is further discussion or further action, up to and including leaving the organization, required if the change we feel is so important is not made? Whatever the case, we will be more consciously engaged. By following the requirements of

Corollary 7, we will be learning more about the organization (its openness to change, for example). And we will be learning more about ourselves (e.g., our ability to present our case, to create solutions, to adapt and change as warranted).

> **Corollary 8:**
> **It is ethical to create organizational improvements. These improvements may be in the form of or result in increased revenue, decreased costs, improved services, or an enhanced organizational culture. But whatever the form or result, it is unethical not to help the organization evolve.**

According to philosopher and ethicist John David Garcia, nothing so increases our own creativity as does the effort to increase the creativity of another.[3] And what does it mean to create organizational improvements or to help an organization evolve if not, at some level and in some way, to increase the creativity of others who are either in the organization or affected by it?

And what in organizational life cannot be improved? Opportunities are everywhere. A given improvement may result in an enhanced organizational culture, a place where good ideas and good works are recognized and motivation is high because the sense of meaningful involvement and meaningful return is high. Or an improvement may directly benefit the bottom line, creating an expansion of the market through the development of new and improved products and services. Or improvement can be made in the nature and structure of the organization itself, its vision for itself, the way leadership is exercised, the distribution of ownership or labor. Whatever the improvement, creativity is required, and the result, potentially, is an increase in the creativity of others.

An organization in which its members are looking for and experimenting with improvements of any sort is an organization that is evolving, an organization that very likely has a competitive edge. Such an organization does not necessarily remain accommodating to all members and all consumers. With innovation comes change. However, the likelihood of the organization remaining a good fit for a given member is, in part, a function of that member's ability to meet the requirements of this corollary.

Bring about improvements in which you believe and the fit between you and your organization, other things being equal, will improve.

Even if the improvements we attempt to implement are not adopted, and increasingly, the organization does not evolve in the direction that is right for us, we nevertheless serve ourselves by adhering to the requirements of this corollary. This is the second part of Garcia's logic. We are changed by our effort to evolve the organization. Our creativity is increased as we work to increase the creativity of others. Consider the specific ways in which this is so. By our effort, we deepen our knowledge and understanding of the organization and of organizations in general. We learn how to work all the more effectively within a network of mixed and competing interests, discovering perhaps how to overcome our resistances, our impedances, increasing our flexibility as we learn to let go and get on with what is relevant. We learn about our current limits, our capacity to do what we say should be done. And we learn that it is possible to expand our capacity through persistence on behalf of a change in which we believe. It is true that our efforts can result in a more effective and creative organization. But that is only half of it. We also are the benefactor of our efforts—because whether or not the organization incorporates our improvements, we emerge with a greater capacity to create and thus with a greater belief in our own ability to establish a beneficial rapport with the world around us whether we stay in the organization we are trying to improve or not.

Corollary 9:
It is ethical to protect and defend the organization against destructive influences such as outside forces or internal decision-making practices that lead to fraud, libel, or abuse. It is unethical to remain silent in the face of perceived threats to the organization's survival.

The organization that is free of self-destructive activity (fraud, libel, abuse, negligence, theft, etc.) is an organization that is more likely to survive and prosper. Thus, if organizational members speak up (albeit sensitively, discreetly, creatively) as soon as threats to organizational survival are detected, then the organization has the opportunity to steer clear of danger with greater ease and less expense. This means that energy is freed for innovation—energy that would not be available if the organization was immersed in legal battles over destructive activity that remained undetected for too long. So, from the organization's point of view, behavior in accord with Corollary 9 is essential to long-term organizational success.

From the individual's point of view, Corollary 9 requires a willingness to address situations that may vary from the uncomfortable to the frightening. To face these situations and behave ethically is a measure of the degree to which we are able to put fear aside and act on principle. Garcia draws the line in no uncertain terms: "Never, under any circumstances, knowingly cooperate with or aid any potential client or associate who is engaged in any way in a destructive enterprise. Be uncompromising in this even if it appears that lack of cooperation will lead to economic or physical disaster for you. This last possibility is almost always an illusion, induced by fear."[4]

This corollary, like the previous corollaries, invites us to behave as if we own the organization, as if we are partners in the enterprise, recognizing that our welfare is linked to the welfare of the organization. For the sake of our families, for example, we are hard put to stand by as our organizations (e.g., our workplaces) are weakened by what we believe are illegal or unethical acts. Whistle-blowing is an extreme example, and it does have its place. And certainly, society owes much to those who have had the strength to blow the whistle when all other methods failed. However, much trouble, much entrenchment of organizationally destructive activity, can be corrected if individuals speak up as soon as they sense the need to do so (a theme to which we will return in Ethic 6). It is our willingness to go along with what we fear may not be in our own best interests, or in the best interests of the organization, that is so damaging. By remaining silent, we create the conditions that make heroic efforts necessary.

So, to speak up when issues arise, to hold oneself accountable for doing so, and, thus, to hold the organization accountable to its own mission and purpose, is to give the organization its conscience and thus the mechanism that allows it to detect drift and correct course before there is reason for whistle-blowing, let alone, if it is occurring, additional subterfuge or cover-up.

Corollary 10:
It is ethical to leave an organization whose purpose and values conflict with your own. It is unethical to remain in an organization that requires you to violate your values or personal code of ethics.

With each of the corollaries for Ethic 1, there is benefit for both the organization and the individual. This is true of Corollary 10, as well. The organization prospers most when it is comprised of individuals who believe in its purpose and values. It falters when it is comprised of individuals who find themselves at odds with its purpose and values. To remain in a situation in which our values and ethics are in conflict with those of the organization—where we no longer believe in the prospect of change from within, where our energy for the exercise of the previous corollaries has been exhausted—is to harm the organization. The organization can never reach its potential without the whole-hearted support of those who comprise it.

Similarly, for our self-respect as well as our health, it is vital that we belong to and serve organizations we believe in, not ones that would have us violate our values or personal code of ethics. The fact that we are serving an organization we do not believe in will not and cannot escape our notice. Eventually, it will cause our health as well as our self-esteem to suffer. On the other hand, to serve an organization in which we do believe is empowering. There is a right order and a right livelihood in that arrangement, an alignment with our desire to focus, serve, and create. There are those who may say, "Wait a minute! I can't leave the organization just because by staying I violate my values and personal code of ethics! I've got bills to pay and a family to feed!" And it certainly may be true that you cannot leave immediately. But you can begin to explore your possibilities and perhaps in the process discover that you are capable of creating a way out, and of doing so responsibly, honoring both yourself and the organization as you proceed. To work our way out of an undesirable situation and into a desirable one is enormously empowering, undercutting the notion that we are not capable of creating something better for ourselves. It builds a lasting self-esteem, making visible to ourselves and others our unwillingness to settle for a situation that does not fit our need to both contribute and grow.

"Human beings are perhaps never more frightening than when they are convinced beyond doubt that they are right."

—Sir Lauren van der Post
South African Author

"Piston slap may indeed sound like loose tappets, so to be a good mechanic you have to be constantly attentive to the possibility that you may be mistaken. This is an ethical virtue."

—Matthew B. Crawford
Shop Class as Soulcraft

"To become aware of what is happening, I must pay attention with an open mind. I must set aside my personal prejudices or bias. Prejudiced people see only what fits those prejudices."

—John Heider
The Tao of Leadership

". . . full unfoldment of creativity requires the ending of rigidity."

—David Bohm and F. David Peat
Science, Order, and Creativity

Ethic 2

The Open-Mindedness Ethic[5]

It is ethical to be open to the possibility that your view is incomplete, capable of expansion and improvement. It is unethical to ignore information that could allow you to grow as a person.

The Open-Mindedness Ethic embraces the notion that openness to input, to other views, to novelty, is essential for personal growth. It calls on us to remain curious about life, to consider among other things how we might perform our duties to ourselves and to others more effectively. And it helps ensure an expanding awareness by defining one aspect of the attitude or life-stance that invites that expansion. At base, the Open-Mindedness Ethic is about the cost we pay when awareness ceases to expand and, instead, hardens or calcifies.

It is important to note that Ethic 2 has as its companion Ethic 3, the Deliberate Action Ethic. Though considered separately, one without the other is incomplete.

Ethic 2 acknowledges the partialness of all views.[6] No one knows the whole story. All views are incomplete. Thus, Ethic 2 requires that we temper our certainty with some degree of doubt so that there can remain reason for experimentation, for acquiring new experience, for considering alternative or novel formulations. It is with this ethic that we counter the rigidity of mind that is the enemy of—in fact the exact opposite of—creative thought and creative work.

In practical terms, this means a willingness to consider the input we receive from others. This does not mean that we act on all the input we receive—only that we are open to it. There of course will be many instances when time does not permit the consideration of other views and we find we must decide right now in accord with how we see things currently (see Ethic 3). But until that time (and immediately after that time), Ethic 2 and the openness it requires define the appropriate stance.

The two corollaries that follow may not rise to the level of corollaries. They are here because they offer guidance concerning the further implementation and value of Ethic 2. When the time to act has not yet come, when there remains time to work with others on the creation of an environment that supports the creative advance of those within it, then the following two corollaries offer guidance.

> **Corollary 1:**
> **When seeking a more complete formulation or a difficult-to-find solution, it is of course helpful to ask others what they think. But it is also helpful to precede your own view with phrases that leave open the possibility that you may not be right, phrases like: "As I see it now," or "My experience in these matters leads me to conclude…" Such phrases qualify the finality of whatever follows and leave room for creative problem solving. It is unethical to speak so as to deny creative input from others.**

How we speak to one another influences our willingness to share ideas. To speak as though we are absolutely certain of our position can discourage others from sharing their own differing views, at least in a noncombative way. Within most organizations, absolute certainty (e.g., "This is the way it is!" "I'm right!" "Case closed!") can lead to withdrawal or even resentment on the part of others. On the other hand, to speak in a way that reflects openness invites others to put forward their ideas. This creates a context within which it is easier to find and/or create solutions.

Note: The style of speaking or interacting that invites others to share the best of what they know and are may vary from the one suggested here. With trust, individuals evolve ways of interacting that on the surface might not appear to invite creative exchange—styles that may be dressed in certainty and posturing. But for the individuals involved, they are styles that heighten the creative process, or that cut short formality. These are the creative, playful, even theatrical—but always trust-laden—interaction styles of longtime friends or colleagues. In the absence of that trust, however, or when in doubt, the straightforward openness and invitation of input called for by this corollary represent the fallback position.

The point of this ethic (and its accompanying corollaries) is that without some openness, without some doubt concerning the certainty of our position, knowledge cannot advance. Science, for example, proceeds on the assumption that what we know is partial and incomplete. New information can lead to a revision of our view, to its enlargement or advance. In this way, our understanding expands. Openness to new information is the key—openness to the possibility that our view is incomplete and might be in error.

> **Corollary 2:**
> **It is ethical to be open to the possibility that you yourself, or some unknown factor, may be responsible—however minutely—for the undesirable events that come your way. It is unethical to presume absolute certainty concerning the failure or fault of others. Such absolute certainty can obscure or cut short the examination of other factors and lead to destructive action against individuals rather than to one's growth as a person.**

By leaving open the possibility that it might be us or other factors, and not the other person, who is truly and totally at fault, we force an examination of our own behavior. Instead of closing the issue by affixing blame, we explore ways in which we might increase our effectiveness and perhaps our wholeness. By this corollary, we are encouraged to look for and eliminate our blind spots, recognizing that on occasion we ourselves produce the undesirable events that come our way, however unconsciously.

Further, by focusing some part of our energy and analysis on ourselves rather than laboring to affix blame, we increase the likelihood that beneficial changes will follow. Encountering the same problem—to the extent that it is due to previously unidentified or perhaps unconscious factors—becomes less likely as we change what we are doing, no longer behaving in ways that invite the problem or make us vulnerable to it. Actions against individuals may be necessary. Specific individuals may be sufficiently responsible for some undesirable or damaging event. If so, then the proper sanctioning will need to occur. But by following the guidance of this corollary, we increase the likelihood that we will not miss the opportunity, should it exist, to expand our awareness and make needed personal improvements.

"... only deliberate action ... is distinctively moral."

—John Dewey
American Philosopher
Morals and Conduct

"As I said to you when you were going away, take care also of his brother Apollodorus. [He] causes me anxiety when he does what he does not mean to do."

—Epicurus
Greek Philosopher, Third Century BC
Fragments

"The first thing to do in life is to do with purpose what one proposes to do."

—Pablo Casals
Cellist

Ethic 3

The Deliberate Action Ethic

It is ethical to choose consciously and execute deliberately specific actions that you believe represent the best of your discernible options. When the time to act has come, it is unethical to not do something.

Ethic 3 is the companion to Ethic 2. Each is incomplete without the other. For however desirable and appropriate the openness of Ethic 2, the time to act does come. And when it comes, it is to the requirements of the act that we must turn (even though our view is necessarily incomplete according to Ethic 2).

Of course, each of us is left with deciding when the time to act has come, and left also with choosing what to do if the time is now.[7] Therein lies our dilemma, and our freedom. Ethic 3 acknowledges and emphasizes our responsibility to ourselves and to others when it states that when the time to act has come, we must choose to do something.[8] We must make a conscious decision and proceed (even if that decision is to withdraw rather than intervene, in a sense to do nothing). To fail to consciously choose to do something is to stand by idly when the opportunity for personal growth presents itself. We are made in such moments (a topic to be discussed in more detail in Part III); or, rather, we make ourselves in such moments, and we make the organizations of which we are a part. What we choose to do when the time to act comes is everything—or leads to everything—and so, our choices must be increasingly conscious. Ethic 3, which on the surface seems so obvious, is an acknowledgment and honoring of our role as agents in the creation of ourselves as persons, our organizations, and society overall.

In everyday life, the actual play of Ethics 2 and 3 and the requirements or standards they impose is such that one ethic may never operate in the total absence of the other. While acting (Ethic 3), there remains openness to new information, and this new information may influence the next decision, the next action. This, no doubt, is how it is and how it must be in order to maximize the transaction between self and world. Emergencies do arise, requiring a focus and concentration that leave little awareness for anything other than the essentials of the act itself. The policeman, the fireman, the surgeon, the soldier, the parent all find themselves in situations that call for concentrated, immediate action, for decisions that must be based on what has been learned up to that very moment. At the same time, it is to our advantage, and to the advantage of those who will be affected by what we do, to remain as open as possible, as conscious as possible, as sensitive as possible, throughout the execution of the act (that is, throughout the long chain of behaviors that may constitute the act) so that our decision-making can reflect the latest turn of events. In this way, we make it less likely that we will proceed unconsciously at a time when openness to new information would call for a new or different course of action.

The tendency that this ethic (and its companion, Ethic 2) works to counter is the tendency to be unconscious, to become habit-and/or rule-governed, turning everyday life over to the robot-self. The presumption of Ethic 3 is that we are consciously deciding our way forward, piloting and navigating as opposed to simply and unconsciously living out the dictates of past conditioning.

Augusto Boal, the Brazilian theatrical scholar, writes about how we can allow "the repetitive acts of daily life" to put us to sleep—how we can "perform the play of breakfast, the scene of going to work, the act of working, the epilogue of supper, the epic of Sunday lunch with the family, etc., like actors in a long run of a successful show, repeating the same lines to the same partners, executing the same movements, at the same times, thousands of times over. Life . . . [becoming] a series of mechanizations, as rigid and as lifeless as the movements of a machine."[9] The result is that we can become sleepwalkers, unmotivated by and unable to act on the requirements of our own development—unmotivated, period. When in this condition, we are on hold, hypnotized by the sameness of everyday life and no longer present or available to the requirements and possibilities of the moment.

On the other hand, to be open to the requirements and possibilities of the moment, whatever they are (the needs/requirements of the body, of others, of the organization, of our own creative callings) and in response to execute the best of our discernible options, is to make ourselves present and engaged. That is ethical. To not act when, clearly, the time to act has come is unethical. And the sad fact is that often the time to act is long overdue and still we have not acted, preferring sleep, hypnosis, the state of being on hold, to the challenge of our own development. Never mind that the course called for by Ethic 3 is time and trouble saving. Never mind that it puts us in the best position to minimize our errors and to learn from them. These benefits are up against habit and fear, a rigidity costing us our capacity to create and, eventually, our self-esteem.

Ethics 2 and 3 call for a life stance characterized by openness and, when the time to act has come, by decisiveness; a stance characterized by the conscious choosing and executing of the best of what we know to do. It is a stance in service to the creative development of ourselves as persons. It is not all that is required of us, and it is not easy, but only by means of this stance do we remain self-directing and, thus, in a position to learn from our experience while thoughtfully and deliberately adding to it.

". . . everything has a tendency to deteriorate. One of the important things leaders need to learn is to recognize the signals of impending deterioration."

—Max DePree
Leadership Is an Art

". . . no system can operate humanely without adequate feedback."

—Philip Slater
Earthwalk

"A man cannot speak but he judges himself . . . Every opinion reacts on him who utters it."

—Ralph Waldo Emerson
American Philosopher
Compensation

Ethic 4

The Feedback Ethic[10]

It is ethical to request, encourage, and deliver feedback. It is unethical to ignore or discourage feedback.

Only with feedback are we able to develop, learn, self-correct, and self-regulate. Only with feedback do we know if we are on or off course. Thus, Ethic 4 emphasizes our duty to ourselves and to others to make sure that feedback is encouraged, delivered, and responded to effectively so that development occurs and desired ends are reached.

Perhaps nothing so characterizes the mature adult as does the ability to give and receive feedback. It is nearly an art form. To give feedback in a fashion that is authentic, without diminishment or blame, tailored to the individual and inviting of his or her development, is a notable skill. And just as notable is the ability to accept feedback, to invite it, and then, when it arrives, to respond constructively, turning the feedback, however it is delivered, to the advantage of oneself and others.

Philosopher John David Garcia writes, "The essential thing in any game is to have a strategy that enables us to learn from our mistakes as well as from our successes. When this is the case, we cannot help but improve our strategies every time we play the game. Self-improving strategies are only possible when there is feedback."[11] For Garcia, in order to fully utilize feedback, we must put aside fear and defensiveness. Truth must be valued over happiness, and personal development and the development of others valued over things as they are. Only then can the information contained in the feedback be used to full advantage.

The following corollaries expand Ethic 4 into its component themes. Two of the corollaries make specific reference to the use of feedback within the workplace. However, as the text attempts to make clear, they are not limited to that setting.

Corollary 1:
It is ethical to request and encourage feedback on your performance, product(s), and materials from individuals with whom you interact and/or who, in one way or another, receive your services, whether they are inside or outside the organization. It is unethical to ignore or discourage feedback.

Only with feedback can we improve our performance. Without it, we lack the information needed for correction and refinement. If what we are doing is what customers/consumers/audiences/loved ones desire, then their feedback will fortify us, giving us confidence in the course we have taken. If what we are doing is not what they desire, then their feedback will alert us to that fact and perhaps offer us information on how we might improve. Either way, the feedback we receive serves us.

To request and encourage feedback is a tangible way of expressing respect for those we serve, whether they are inside or outside the organization. Responding constructively to the feedback we receive in turn promotes respect. By our response, those providing the feedback witness their presence in the change process. They see that they can affect the course of things and that the person or organization with which they are dealing is open to change.

Similarly, to respond constructively to the feedback we receive from friends and loved ones is to announce that their opinions matter, and that we matter to ourselves as well—so much so that we will change what we are doing if there are benefits to doing so. This is self-and other-respecting, and it invites respect. It models a standard that reflects a commitment to personal growth and makes clear that living up to such a standard is not at all unrealistic but entirely doable.

This corollary does not imply that we must act on the feedback we receive. The feedback we receive may not be useful. It does imply, however, that we must invite feedback and that we must not ignore or discourage it when it is offered. While the feedback we receive may not be helpful this time, the feedback we receive next time may be extremely helpful. However, if we have ignored, discouraged, or in some way punished the person from whom we are receiving feedback, then we reduce the likelihood of a next time. Thus, it is self-and organizationally-destructive to ignore or discourage feedback, healthy to invite feedback, to be open and alert to what it might offer.[12]

Corollary 2:
It is ethical to offer feedback to those from whom you receive services. It is ethical to acknowledge outstanding performance, just as it is ethical to provide feedback to those whose performance or service threatens the optimal performance of you or your organization. In both cases, it may be unethical not to do so.

Corollary 1 emphasizes the importance of inviting and encouraging feedback. Corollary 2 emphasizes the importance of *giving* feedback. Indeed, we have an obligation to give feedback if circumstances require it. By giving feedback, we provide information others may find useful in their effort to fine-tune their performance or achieve their desired ends. Thus, one of the most important skills we ever acquire is the ability to give feedback effectively; that is, sincerely, nondefensively, without apology, anger, or blame.

Acknowledging outstanding performance, for example, or the next advance over past performance (as in the arts of teaching, parenting, and team-building), is the hallmark of a positive culture. In a positive culture, individuals are on the lookout for quality or for what might, with persistence, turn into quality. They are on the lookout for the striving that serves development. And when they see it, they acknowledge it, knowing that a positive culture is of service to all within it. In such a culture, individuals experience support for what they do well (or are attempting to do well) and, increasingly, they are in touch with their desire to realize their developmental potential. They feel safer and more empowered than they otherwise would because they are in a culture interested in seeing the best of what they have to offer.

When given correctly (as discussed in more detail in Corollary 3), feedback requires a concern for the other person while, at the same time, maintaining an allegiance to one's principles. This is particularly true for critical or negative feedback. Individuals who can deliver negative feedback are invaluable to their organizations because they do not compound problems as they work to correct them. They know how to give feedback without indictment or blame and, so, how to remove from the recipient of the feedback the excuse to blame the messenger. This is the way in which feedback, when properly given, helps the individual assume responsibility for her behavior. It allows and encourages the individual to consider the potential relevance of what is being said. Feedback delivered in this way is a service to the individual and to the organization and, coincidently, serves as a measure of one's own growth. To deliver feedback sensitively, creatively, while remaining true to the mission of the organization and to one's own standards and principles, is to give evidence of one's own capacity to stay on course even in the face of potentially turbulent or uncomfortable exchanges.[13]

Finally, it is possible in organizations (whether two-person "organizations" or larger) to feel unseen or unheard. Corollaries 1 and 2 make this condition increasingly unlikely because they encourage a give-and-take on matters relevant to organizational health and performance. The sense of not being connected or meaningfully involved is obviated by these corollaries since they call on us to take responsibility for our own sense of involvement. Corollary 1 states (in effect): Invite connection by inviting feedback. You thereby announce your presence in the organization—i.e., your willingness to be critiqued, your respect for the opinion of others, your desire to be connected. Corollary 2 states (again, in effect): Give feedback to others. Confirm their efforts, offer advice (if it seems appropriate to do so), and establish connections by speaking to matters relevant to the organization. Also, speak up if feedback is not coming your way. Give feedback on the absence of feedback to avoid colluding silently with the absence of a practice essential to personal and organizational effectiveness. In this way, the degree to which we are seen and heard, the degree to which we feel connected and involved, is ours to affect.

If, after all our efforts (in accord with Corollaries 1 and 2), feedback and a sense of connection are still not forthcoming, then that is feedback of another sort: feedback that casts doubt on the worthiness of the organization and our affiliation with it. Or (and this must always be a consideration) it is feedback on the skill with which we request and offer feedback. It is always possible that our manner, our way of asking for and offering feedback, is threatening, insincere, blaming, and/or not constructive or truly welcoming (hence the need for Corollary 3).

> **Corollary 3:**
> **It is ethical to deliver feedback sensitively and to accept it graciously. It is unethical to diminish the person to whom you are giving feedback or to punish the person from whom you are receiving it.**

"Double vision"—the poet William Blake's term—is the capacity to see a thing in at least two ways simultaneously. It springs from the realization that what we choose to see (or hear or sense) is but one of many things that can be seen (or heard or sensed). This leads to the conclusion that what is seen reveals as much about us and what we value as it does about what is available to be seen. In a similar way, what we identify as worthy of feedback may reveal as much about us and what we value as it does about the person to whom we are giving the feedback. We may or may not be serving the values of the organization or the best interests of all concerned. "A man cannot speak but he judges himself," said Emerson, "Every opinion reacts on him who utters it." For this reason, it is important to give feedback sensitively and to accept it graciously, realizing—as Garcia points out—that the feedback we give may be in error (i.e., more about ourselves than the other person), while the feedback we receive may be correct.

Further, to diminish those to whom we give feedback or to punish those from whom we receive it is self-destructive. In the first instance, the feedback we give will not be heard since the individual is likely to focus on the diminishment and not on the content of the feedback. (For the individual receiving the feedback, the diminishment *is* the content!) And in the second instance, the person from whom we are receiving the feedback is less likely to offer feedback in the future if the current effort to do so is punished. Only after the issue has worsened might the individual again attempt to offer us feedback and then, possibly, with resentment that he must do so at all. Either way, to diminish the person to whom we are giving feedback or to punish the person from whom we are receiving it is to make the culture of the organization or the relationship between the two parties increasingly hostile. Only individuals committed to their own growth can rise above this hostility, if it does develop, and continue to give and receive feedback constructively regardless of how the feedback was delivered to them or received by others.

Again, as indicated earlier, familiarity and fondness can lead to idiosyncratic, tailored, even theatrical or playful modes of exchanging feedback. To the outside observer, these modes may seem insensitive. But the feedback is heard and the obligation to give feedback is not avoided. No affront is taken. An established relationship can permit kindness or regard for the other person to shine through an unorthodox delivery. There is sensitivity and grace in this, as well as love, even though the style departs from what is recommended here. The corollary is not violated; rather, it is expressed creatively. When in doubt, however, when there is not a bond or familiarity or trust, the more formal and careful delivery of feedback, along with the more obviously gracious acceptance of it, is the preferred mode. With this mode, the trust, fondness, and respect so essential to the richness that is interpersonal and organizational life can evolve.

Finally, the work of Robert Kegan and Lisa Laskow Lahey is instructive with respect to the delivery of feedback.[14] Kegan and Lahey looked into what they called the "language of ongoing regard" and offered the following instruction: When offering feedback, "be direct, be specific, and be nonattributive." Don't dissipate the impact of your feedback by being indirect. Speak directly to the person to whom you are giving feedback and be specific about what it is that has caused you to speak up. Avoid characterization, the ascribing of attributes. The person to whom you are giving feedback knows (or feels she knows) how wonderful (or generous or kind or angry or peaceful) she is. For you to say that she is so wonderful invites her to assess herself and say (to herself, if not to you): "No, I am not really so wonderful (or angry or generous)." By ascribing an attribute, we define the person. And the person, who knows herself better than we do, reacts by deciding how correct we are. If, instead, we share our experience with the person—what she leads us to experience—we take away the inclination to judge us right or wrong. After all, it is our experience; how could we be wrong? This provides what Kegan and Lahey call "a precious kind of information," information on the individual's impact on the world, information the individual can use to define herself.[15]

"So I went to studying it out. I says to myself, I reckon a body that ups and tells the truth when he is in a tight place is taking considerable many resks, though I ain't had no experience, and can't say for certain; but it looks so to me, anyway; and yet here's a case where I'm blest if it don't look to me like the truth is better and actually SAFER than a lie. I must lay it by in my mind, and think it over some time or other, it's so kind of strange and unregular. I never seen nothing like it."

—Mark Twain
The Adventures of Huckleberry Finn

" . . . most people opt for a life of very limited honesty and openness and relative closedness, hiding themselves and their maps from the world . . . [Those who tell the truth] are not burdened by any need to hide . . . They do not have to construct new lies to hide old ones."

—M. Scott Peck
The Road Less Traveled

". . . my driving conviction is that all humanity is in peril of extinction if each one of us does not dare, now and henceforth, always to tell only the truth and all of the truth, and to do so promptly—right now."

—Buckminster Fuller
Critical Path

Ethic 5

The Truth-Telling Ethic

It is ethical to tell the truth, to be honest. Truth-telling promotes clarity and allows you to match resources with greater precision to the demands of the moment. It is unethical to lie. Lying creates misinformation, confusion, and distrust, threatening your ability to survive, adapt, and prosper.

The Truth-Telling Ethic states that it is ethical to tell the truth, to be honest. It goes without saying that here we are talking about the truth as we know it, the truth of our experience, in accord with our own sense of principle and privacy. Obviously, there are certain questions the answers to which are no one's business but our own, as well as comments we could make that would serve only to hurt or damage others. We do not answer some questions and we do not express some views, however true we may believe them to be, because to do so would serve no purpose but to harm others.

Here, with this ethic as elsewhere with the ethics of human development, there are exceptions. Obviously if by telling the truth we would put someone's life in danger or hurt their feelings unnecessarily, we make an exception. But making exceptions is a tricky business. We should not make exceptions for personal gain or convenience. Only if the individual cannot utilize the truth constructively for personal growth are we justified in withholding it. And making such a judgment requires a discernment of such an exalted degree that only genuine love for the other can drive it. This was M. Scott Peck's point in his book *The Road Less Traveled*, and having made this point he cautions, " . . . in assessing the capacity of another to utilize the truth for personal/spiritual growth, it should be borne in mind that our tendency is generally to underestimate rather than overestimate this capacity."[16]

Will Schutz, one of the founders of the human potential movement, offered the following:

> Honesty and openness are the keys to your evolutionary growth. Being honest allows your bodymind to become a clear channel for taking in all the energy of the universe, both inside and outside your body, and to use it profitably. You must spend great amounts of energy to hide your feelings, thoughts, or wishes from other people, and even more energy to keep them from yourself. To withhold secrets requires a tightened body; it requires vigilance, shallow breathing, physical exertion and a preoccupation with your own safety. This results in your missing all sorts of stimuli because your bodymind is not relaxed enough to allow them in.[17]

When we lie, we have to keep track of what we said. Otherwise, we run the risk of being found out. This means that the memory and mental capacity that we would otherwise have available are instead devoted to keeping things straight. By definition, then, to lie is to diminish the resources available for creative pursuits. On the other hand, to tell the truth, one's own truth, without compromise, but with the open-mindedness of Ethic 2, is to serve the cause of clarity. Perspective is furthered. As Schutz points out, truth-telling or honesty helps ensure "a clear channel for taking in all the energy of the universe," a "bodymind" less cluttered, less noisy, less divided, and thus more present and available to the creative opportunities of the moment. At base, truth-telling announces the individual's interest not in manipulating others, not in hiding or self-protection, but in personal growth.

For this reason, the decision to abide by the Truth-Telling Ethic is one of the most important decisions we ever make. It is the decision to embrace life as it is, not as we would embellish it; a decision to accept what experience and current reasoning tells us is so and, thus, a decision not to perpetuate the party line, however convenient or self-serving it would be to do so. With this ethic, the individual commits his development to a principle, believing that a shorter, more direct route to understanding exists, a route that calls for the voicing of one's truth in situations that matter, withholding it—if at all—only out of regard for the welfare of others.

In organizations, truth-telling and honesty go hand in hand with organizational health. Without truth-telling, without the telling of difficult but necessary truths, the organization and its members cannot identify and address their problems. Nor can they build the trust needed for personal and organizational effectiveness. With trust comes possibility. Without trust, all parties find themselves immersed in second-guessing. Of course, there are times within organizations when the truth might need to be withheld. But for those individuals intent on finding exceptions, it is important to remember that when it is learned that the truth has been withheld, the trust that is broken will remain broken unless it can be concluded that genuine concern for the other, and not personal gain, was the motive.[18]

Finally, to lie, to withhold the truth, to break the trust among friends, loved ones, colleagues, and associates, to so act without justification, is to betray. And betrayal, when discovered, is profoundly shocking, a blow to the solar plexus. When we discover we have been betrayed, we feel outraged. But we also feel dishonored and shamed. And while we can blame the other person for what they have done to us, often (and for the longest time) we may also blame ourselves. It is possible to so internalize our experience of betrayal—depending on its severity and the age at which it occurs—that it shakes our sense of self-worth for a lifetime. "What is it about me that invites this dishonoring? I must not be worthy," we may conclude. However in error this conclusion, it nevertheless can characterize the inner dialogue of the individual—the child, for example, or the young adult—who turns on themselves as if they were deserving of the betrayal they received.

There is also shame if we are the person who has done the betraying. Whether betrayer or betrayed, we can find our experience "de-spiriting." And one of the dangers is that we will use our experience as an excuse for engaging in more of the same. "It's a dog-eat-dog world," we might think. "Look out for yourself. It was done to me; I can do it to others. It's part of the game." In this way, an organizational culture unravels and so, too, personal relationships.

Or we can take a stand against our lack of fortitude, doing so because the pain of a situation lacking truth-telling and honesty is too great. There is no growth in such a situation, no unfolding of inherent possibilities. And that, ultimately, is painful. And while calling a stop to it could prove difficult, perhaps even painful in the short run, it is nevertheless a step in service to one's development as a person. With this step, the individual opts for a "bodymind" less cluttered and less divided, more the clear channel of which Schutz spoke, opting in effect for relationships and organizational affiliations that support creative involvement and personal growth.

"Whenever smart and well-intentioned people avoid confronting obstacles, they disempower employees and undermine change."

—John P. Kotter
Leading Change

" . . . Everything we shut our eyes to, everything we run away from, everything we deny, denigrate or despise, serves to defeat us in the end. What seems nasty, painful, evil, can become a source of beauty, joy and strength, if faced with an open mind."

—Henry Miller
Twentieth-Century American Writer

Ethic 6

The Pain-Directed Ethic

It is ethical in ongoing personal and organizational development to work first on the issue causing the most pain, then to work on the next most painful issue, and so on, in this way creating improvements in the sequence most likely to ensure not only survival but also health and wellbeing. It is unethical to ignore painful issues. By ignoring painful issues, we allow them to compound, threatening all the more the ability of the person or organization to accomplish his or its purpose.

Nothing so retards development as the willingness to escape from and/or avoid difficult and painful issues. When we use such stratagems (escape and avoidance), the painful issues never go away. Instead, they worsen, all the more inclining us toward escape and avoidance until at last the issue becomes a crisis that must be addressed if we are to avert disaster.

To put it another way, the painful and difficult issues that confront us, whether as individuals or within our organizations, rarely emerge fully blown. For the most part, they start out small and then grow because instead of dealing with them when first noticed, we turn away, only to discover when we turn back days, weeks, or months later that they have compounded and now require far more of us than would have been the case had we dealt with them initially.

The Pain-Directed Ethic attempts to eliminate escape and avoidance from the management style of self and organization. It asks us to identify what is not working both in our lives and in our part of our organizations and then calls on us to address the most severe of these—the issue that represents the greatest threat to our ability or our organization's ability to accomplish our/its purpose. And when that issue or problem is resolved, or when all that can be done today has been done, to move to the next most severe problem, and so on. In this way, the entity in question, whether self or organization, is brought with maximum speed to a more smoothly functioning, integrated whole, and kept there.

Leadership is distinguished by this ethic, by its willingness to face issues as they arise rather than putting off the duty to their organization because of fear or inconvenience. Some of the best organizational leaders begin their tenure by asking: What is the greatest threat to our organization's ability to accomplish its purpose, the issue that is—in that sense—causing the most pain? And they proceed amidst their other everyday duties to make that item their number one organizational development priority. When that issue has been addressed, or as the plan to address it is underway, the next most serious or painful issue is identified and addressed, and so on, until the issues that must be faced are, on average, smaller and less intractable, and so require less time and energy to address.

It was this ethic that Gandhi spoke to with his admonition: "Do what is right, now!"—that is, do not procrastinate. Address the painful issue now, before it compounds and becomes more painful still. And it was Lao Tsu, the Taoist philosopher, who expressed the benefit implicit in the embracing of this ethic when he wrote, "Because the sage always confronts difficulties, he never experiences them"[19]—which is to say, he confronts them as soon as they are detected, when they are hardly difficulties at all.

With that said, several additional points concerning this ethic are worth making. First, it is true that some issues in one's life or in organizations have been ignored for so long that they have become mountains, the prospect of scaling them overwhelming. To deal with these issues, a capacity must be developed, perhaps by taking on smaller, less daunting issues first until, with success, a greater capacity emerges. This, in fact, may be the way we address the issue—gradually, by approximation. However, even with this most reasonable of stratagems, we can find that we are avoiding the issue looming before us, an issue that becomes larger with each passing day. Believing that we are building capacity may be the way we trick ourselves into thinking we are addressing the issue when, in fact, it is the clever way we are avoiding it. Clearly, we must work up to some issues, but it is also important to remember that once engaged with what we know we must address, we often find we have more capacity than we had presumed. The requirements associated with putting things right take over, and we discover abilities we thought we lacked.

Of course, in accordance with Ethic 2, we must be open to the possibility that we may be wrong about the nature of the problem before us. This is always possible. However, only by attempting to deal constructively with what we believe to be the problem do we begin to narrow in on its true nature. We may discover that what we thought was the problem was in fact an outcropping, a symptom, and not the real problem at all, our effort serving only to improve our understanding. We are always in danger of misjudgment, of acting in error. And yet only by proceeding with the requirements of the Pain-Directed Ethic and the ethics of human development in general can we discover the true nature of the problem before us and how best to address it.

Writer and philosopher Eckhart Tolle provided an analogy that turns this analysis in the direction of the self. Too often, writes Tolle, "We find abhorrent the image we see reflected in the mirror and so, we attack the mirror."[20] We go after the reflection and not its source. The problem is presumed to be out there, and so long as that is the presumption, the problem will remain. What we see out there can be a reflection of what we are doing or failing to do in our everyday lives, in our treatment of ourselves and others. This happens often enough for there to be value in asking whether by some behavior or stance, the problem we face is actually self-caused. This question promotes self-examination and can lead to changes in doing and being that are liberating for both self and organization. Obviously, if there is something wrong in our lives or in our part of the organization, if there is negativity, dysfunction, or pain, then change is required. However, if we are unable to initiate the change, unable to behave in new ways that might bring about the change, continuing to behave as we have in the past even though it has been to no avail, then part of the problem is in us. We are stuck or rigid in ways that conspire to keep things as they are. The Pain-Directed Ethic, by its insistence that painful issues be addressed, leads us on a search for the source of the pain, and sometimes those searches lead back to the self.

So, to ignore a pain-producing issue and our role in solving it is unethical not only because it is self-and organizationally-destructive but because it ignores what may be an opportunity for personal growth. Pain announces that there is a problem in the system. Some part or parts are suffering while other parts remain unaffected for now. The Pain-Directed Ethic requires that we identify the source of the pain, track it down, and resolve it so that the system is no longer under threat. This can lead to a confronting of our fears, our resistances to change, to a confronting of our map of reality—which in turn leads, invariably, to a test of commitment and flexibility. No matter how challenging the issue, however, when we proceed in accord with the requirements of this ethic, we are at least fortified by the relevance of what we are doing. If we are successful in resolving the issue, whatever it is and wherever it lies, then we will have exhibited (and perhaps increased) control over ourselves while at the same time freeing energy for other pursuits.

"Only mutually voluntary transactions can ever be ethical or creative."

—John David Garcia
Creative Transformation

"Bad faith: Seeking to blame someone or something for what one has done freely oneself . . . pretending that one is born . . . determined . . . instead of recognizing that one spends one's life . . . making oneself."

From Hazel E. Barnes' introduction to Jean-Paul Sartre's *Being and Nothingness*

" . . . choice is burdensome and effortful, it requires resolution, a lifting up of the power of personality against the spiritual gravitation of impulse or habit or sloth. Choice is creation, and creation is labor."

—Will Durant
The Story of Philosophy

Ethic 7

The Free Choice Ethic

> ***It is ethical to assume that you are choosing to do all that you do, that you come to your tasks by choice, that you are involved voluntarily with the requirements of your life. It is unethical to assume, unless extreme circumstances prevail, that you are being made or forced to do anything.***[21]

Ethic 7 goes to the heart of the matter, to choice, to what is meant by the term and to why it is so important. None of the ethics discussed thus far, nor any that will be discussed later, stirs so much discomfort. But without choice, there are no ethics. The entire notion of ethics is predicated on the presumption of choice, on the presumption that we are choosing our way forward, our stories composed largely by the choices we make. And yet try telling yourself that you do not actually have to do what you are doing, that no one is forcing you to do what you are doing. In response, you may hear from inside yourself an uproar: "I have no choice!" But most of the time this is not true and should not be assumed to be true. You may dislike your options, but choice—the freedom to accept, create, transcend, or leave—must be assumed or the entire concept of ethics is out the door.

Still, the presumption of choice, though essential, is often unwelcome because it addresses and undercuts our propensity to think of ourselves as victims; our propensity to conclude that our misery, our disgruntlement, was inevitable, forced upon us by forces larger than ourselves (and indifferent at that), our situation determined by the hand we were dealt. In fairness, it can be hard, especially later in life or when things have not gone our way, not to conclude that our biology was our destiny, or that our parents, through their limitations, established our own, launching us on a course from which self-directed departures were largely an illusion. And equally hard at times not to point to class, culture, age, gender, race, or ethnicity as the reasons for our developmental stage, psychologically and spiritually. These are potent and relevant factors. They no doubt affect the range of options available at any point in time. Yet as relevant as they are, and though they must be honored for the uniqueness and diversity they insert into the developmental and evolutionary process, they nevertheless serve only to define the stage whereon we operate, not the outcome. The development of higher character, if it is to occur, remains ours alone, something we are capable of creating through the conscious effort to do so. The Free Choice Ethic encourages us to abandon the victim paradigm and to see the role that choice plays in shaping both consciousness and conduct, with these other factors, potent as they are, saluted for what they contribute but no longer presumed responsible for what we become.

The presumption of choice, however, along with the presumption of being a self-responsible agent, is tricky because, in truth, the self evolves. We do not start out with sufficient awareness to choose and follow through with those options that serve the cause of our own development. We must develop that capacity; as we do so, choice enters our life by degree. With every developmental step, awareness expands and, with it, the capacity to see options, to choose ever more consciously, and so, to exercise responsibility for what we do and become. That is why the ethics of human development and this ethic in particular are not for children. It is for adults and would-be adults who recognize that with the presumption of choice comes the presumption—necessarily and increasingly—of responsibility.[22] These presumptions of choice and responsibility emphasize and help create our role as authors of our own lives, encouraging self-reflection, forethought, and a growth in awareness that leads sooner rather than later to mature, responsible decision-making.

What we are emerging out of as we develop and mature is a life lived unconsciously, a life directed by the programming of the past. What we enter is a life conscious of that programming, conscious of it in all its subtle and profound aspects and, thus, a life in which choice—anchored to reason, principle, and the requirements of further development rather than robotic compliance—can occur. With expanded (and expanding) awareness we see how we have so often proceeded unconsciously in the past. How our current situation is very possibly related to choices we ourselves have made. We begin to take responsibility for our next steps in life as we see options we did not see before. The ethics of human development emphasize education, feedback, and learning, as by those means awareness is expanded. But on a more profound level, as with this ethic in particular, the ethics of human development presume choice, our capacity for self-direction as increasingly integral to our way of operating in the world.

So, with this ethic, choice is presumed—and increasingly so as we develop. Having said that, consider now philosopher Jean-Paul Sartre's notion of "bad faith." Bad faith, in Sartre's philosophy, means "Presuming/pretending/behaving as if what is before us is mandatory when it is, in fact, voluntary."[23] Bad faith is one of the ways we delude ourselves, one of the ways we deny responsibility for the choices we are making. Consider an all-too-common example. Many of us in our day-to-day work lives, in organizations we have chosen to join and from which we are free to exit, approach our tasks as if someone were making us do them, as though we were being forced to do them. Long after joining the organization, perhaps years later, we walk the halls, enter meetings, and undertake work-related duties like captives, pretending that what is before us is mandatory and not voluntary at all. And yet, according to this ethic, we are there by choice, free to exit or in some way modify our experience. To pretend otherwise is disastrous for us and for the organization. It is self-dishonoring, psychologically weakening, and an example of how far we are willing to go to avoid the burden and responsibility implicit in choice—in this case, in choosing to be where we have placed ourselves, or in choosing another way of being there, or in choosing something new.

Which team is more likely to succeed: the team comprised of volunteers or the team comprised of individuals behaving as if they are required to participate? The team comprised of volunteers has the energy, the lack of dividedness, the clarity of purpose to succeed or at least realize its potential. The team comprised of individuals behaving as if they are required to participate merely gets by—or perhaps not even that, since a subtle form of sabotage is often present in this type of team culture as members consciously and unconsciously create excuses for not participating fully.

There are consequences for choosing to participate and for choosing not to participate. There are always consequences. The choice to be a part of a team may or may not be an easy one. But it is our choice nonetheless. The Free Choice Ethic states that you are free to be part of the team or not as you choose. If you are choosing to be on the team, then acknowledge that fact and choose to be there. That does not mean you will not vigorously challenge team practices that you believe hurt the ability of the team to accomplish its purpose. And it does not mean that you will continue to choose to be on the team if, in your view, it is no longer worthy of your involvement. It merely means that if you are choosing to be on the team then be there fully, totally, doing what it takes (within the bounds of your ethical framework) to make the team a success. On the other hand, if you are choosing not to be on the team, then get off. The exercise of bad faith, the denial of your own capacity to create through choice, is destructive and unethical. It is one way to disempower yourself and in the process create work, trouble, and hardship for those around you.

It is true that a more complete analysis of the behavior in question (of the individual who behaves as if he is being forced to do what clearly he is free not to do) includes the fact that at some level the individual feels unseen, unheard, or in some other way disregarded. And so he pouts, expressing resentment or anger in subtle and not-so-subtle ways.[24] (As an aside, this is why the ethics of human development in their entirety point us toward activities that ensure that all are regarded and engaged, thereby helping to ensure that an excuse to exercise bad faith will not be present in the culture.) But to wait to be recognized or embraced by the surrounding culture before behaving in ways that honor one's own development is self-destructive. It places one's dreams and aspirations on hold, allowing the will to atrophy, and thus does nothing to bring about the culture, team, organization, or self that one desires. Even if indifference reigns, even if we remain unseen and ignored, still this ethic tells us we must not pretend we have no choice. Honor yourself and empower yourself by recognizing that you very possibly decided your way into your present situation, a journey of many steps and many choices. And now, if you wish, you can change your situation. You can decide your way out, honorably and ethically, though that, too, may be a journey of many steps and many choices. But do not pretend that the power to affect your situation—or your experience of it—lies solely outside yourself. True, there may be factors outside your control. But the capacity to creatively respond to what is given, to discern and choose the option that can conceivably expand your freedom and/or your development as a person, is yours alone, and increasingly so as you so choose. That is the heart of Ethic 7.

This brings one final point to the surface—or perhaps it is merely a restating of what has been said already. With the presumption of choice and the growing degree of responsibility it implies, there come the most challenging of questions, questions that invite a thoughtful overview, a generous and forgiving self-examination. Who is responsible for your creativity? Who is responsible for the heart and energy you put into your pursuits? Who is responsible for your morale? These questions suggest how far we might go in the application of this ethic to our lives. Whatever our answer to these questions, the Free Choice Ethic pushes us to entertain and even embrace if possible a responsibility that is nearly freedom itself: freedom of spirit, to be exact. Without adherence to this ethic, we cannot travel the full length of the Yellow Brick Road. We pursue the Mature Mind—as described in Part I—through choice, and its achievement is one of the most inspiring of human accomplishments. It is by means of this ethic, with its insistence on extending the reach of our responsibility, that the ethics of human development become the ethics of self-realization.

"It is by not doing what they already know they should do that companies get into trouble over quality."

—Philip B. Crosby
Quality Without Tears

"Anybody possessing analytical knowledge recognizes the fact that the world is full of actions performed by people exclusively to their detriment and without perceptible advantage, although their eyes were open."

—Theodor Reik
Psychoanalyst and Author

" . . . right is right, and wrong is wrong, and a body ain't got no business doing wrong when he ain't ignorant and knows better. It might answer for YOU to dig Jim out with a pick, WITHOUT any letting on, because you don't know no better; but it wouldn't for me, because I do know better."

Tom Sawyer to Huck Finn
—Mark Twain
The Adventures of Huckleberry Finn

Ethic 8

The Conscious Mistakes Ethic

It is ethical to eliminate conscious mistakes. It is unethical to know that what you are about to do is wrong and to do it anyway.

Economist E. F. Schumacher wrote that work exists for the refinement of character.[25] This is one of the tenets to which the ethics of human development is anchored: the notion that work exists for the refinement of character and that work in accord with the ethics of human development refines character, building the capacity for ever-larger motives to be expressed by and through the self.

One measure of this growth in capacity, this refinement of character, is the reduction of conscious mistakes. This refers not to a reduction in mistakes per se—a distinction that should be drawn immediately—but the reduction in *conscious* mistakes.[26] Mistakes, in and of themselves, are one of the ways we learn. Successful individuals often point to the number of mistakes they made until, at last, the successful route was discovered, the invention was made sound, the idea perfected. But no one becomes successful, wise, or more fully integrated by engaging in conscious mistakes. Rather, they and those around them are destroyed, at least by degree.

Perhaps we have misgivings about a given course of action. We think there are problems with it, but overall we believe it to be the course of action we should take, that it is not a mistake to do so. If it turns out to be a mistake rather than the solution or result we had sought, then we will learn from our effort and choose differently next time. With conscious mistakes, however, we already know that the course of action upon which we are about to embark is a mistake, and still, we proceed.

Chuck Berry, the father of rock and roll, said, "Don't let the same dog bite you twice."[27] In so saying, he captured the spirit and reasoning embedded in the Conscious Mistakes Ethic. Many of us, figuratively speaking, can see ourselves in his example: "Many times that dog has bitten me. Indeed, every time I have put my leg inside the fence—even though I have varied my approach, my voice, my dress—every time, he has bitten me. I know it is a mistake to put my leg inside the fence, and yet here I go again!"

While it is self-destructive to engage in conscious mistakes, it is also extremely common to do so. They occur around the dessert tray all the time! They occur around the issue of diet in general, around exercise, relationships, the management of money and time. We may have concluded, for example, that it is a mistake to consume this particular food, this next drink. And still, we eat it or drink it. The body is screaming for exercise. Or perhaps the screaming has died out, and still we know that exercise is needed. Yet we do nothing. This relationship or this job is a mistake and yet we do nothing to change it, modify it, alter it. Instead, we continue with it even though there is no doubt in our mind that as configured, this relationship or job is a mistake. In the world of work, examples abound: "I know it is a mistake not to contact the applicant's references, a mistake not to log my contacts with a given client, a mistake not to talk to my coworker this very day about his performance. But still I do not proceed."

It should be pointed out that none of these examples always fall into the category of conscious mistakes. One person's conscious mistakes are not necessarily another's. Not until we proceed with what we have concluded is a mistake does our conduct fall into this category. Until then, we are doing the best we can, selecting the course of action that in our judgment is not a mistake but, rather, our best option. It is what we know concerning what is right and not right for us in a given situation or with respect to a given issue that determines whether a given choice is a conscious mistake. It is then that this ethic holds us responsible for conduct in accord with that knowledge.

It is the rare person, of course, who can completely eliminate conscious mistakes, just as it is a rare person who lives the totally ethical life. The point of the Conscious Mistakes Ethic is to reduce the frequency and variety of conscious mistakes in the direction of zero, confronting in the process the issues that continue to propel us toward self-destructiveness. *In fact, nothing so deepens the analysis of how we were made, programmed, and/or conditioned as does the effort to figure out why we continue to do what we know we should not do*. Such an analysis takes us back through the history of our development to the processes and events that shaped us, our sense of self, our trust, openness, confidence, our degree of self-regard, back to any and all fundamental confusions that must be addressed if self-love is to prevail. Or perhaps we choose not to go back, but instead to move forward with an attempt to build a new history through conduct anchored to principle rather than past conditioning; conduct that announces that even in that past were the seeds of the breakthrough now in evidence as old, self-destructive patterns are discerned and eliminated. Either way, we are served, consciousness expands, and conscious mistakes are reduced.

One of the problems associated with not addressing and attempting to reduce conscious mistakes is that, through them, we flirt with the hardening of self-destructive habits—habits that, in the extreme, can lead to addiction. If addiction does occur, the problem becomes more complex, so complex that we are often hard put to untangle it alone. Hard put also to consider the addicted individual unethical simply because he continues to do what he knows he should not do. While conscious mistakes are unethical, addiction (which may or may not be the result of one's continuous indulging in conscious mistakes) is a train out of control, a mountain that may or may not be of one's own making but which is enormously difficult to climb. To attempt to climb it—one step at a time, one day at a time, losing ground on some days but returning to climb again—is ethical and self-respecting. Indeed, to seek treatment in such circumstances is ethical. With addiction, a confluence of biological, cultural, and psychological factors operate, all related, perhaps, to an emptiness that must be filled, a craving for wellbeing that got distorted along the way and can now be repaired only gradually, step by step, as the overriding pangs of withdrawal give way to a renewed capacity for self-control.[28]

Conscious mistakes are self-destructive and, in the extreme, can lead to addiction. But they are also organizationally destructive. As we are weakened, so too is every network of which we are a part. But the opposite is equally true: As we grow stronger and become increasingly whole, we bring strength and capacity to every network of which we are a part. If we were once our organization's weakest link, then its weakest link is no longer as weak and so, on the whole, the organization enjoys a new degree of wherewithal. Its center of gravity rises (as will be discussed in Part IV).

Finally, to the extent that one adopts the ethics of human development, to not behave in accord with their requirements is a conscious mistake. In this way, all of the ethics can, in a sense, be reduced to this ethic, this ethic that alone steers conduct and ensures the refinement of character. "Perfection," wrote the writer Ken Carey, "is not the absence of mistakes but rather the absence of conscious mistakes."[29]

"One of the principles which determines our choice of one value over another, is that the permanent should be chosen over the transitory. Conservation, permanence, is a demand growing out of the very nature of value. Again, we say that it is difficult to give any meaning to the life of moral choice and effort, whether in the individual or the race, except on the assumption that there is progress or development towards perfection."

—Wilbur Marshall Urban
Fundamentals of Ethics

Ethic 9

The Sustainability Ethic

It is ethical to consider the long-range implications of your decision-making and to make sustainability a guiding tenet. It is unethical to knowingly implement practices that ensure the collapse or diminished health of the self, the organization, or the environment.

The Sustainability Ethic encourages an awareness that what is done now will have implications for the future—indeed, will build the future for better or worse. So, with this ethic, sustainability is encouraged. Behave so as to preserve and sustain planet Earth and its many interlocking regenerative processes so that this sphere, this spaceship, is kept alive and able to support life's flourishing. That is perhaps this ethic's first requirement. But also preserve and sustain the cultural and personal practices that allow an individual to continue to grow as a person, that keep alive his prospects for further realization, and that keep alive as well his ability to contribute to others safely, constructively, and creatively over the long run. That, too, is a part of the Sustainability Ethic.

The work of systems theorist John Platt on the nature of "traps" and "fences" can be helpful in clarifying the requirements of the Sustainability Ethic.[30] According to Platt, a trap is a situation in which short-term advantage is chosen at the cost of long-term disadvantage, short-term pleasure traded or embraced at the cost of long-term pain.

A personal trap, said Platt, is a situation in which the individual engages in behavior that has immediate or short-term advantages but long-term disadvantages. Examples might include smoking, overeating, eating unhealthy foods, excessive shopping, excessive drinking, criminal activity, perhaps even rudeness or punitive interpersonal tactics—any activity in which the rush, convenience, or pleasure comes with the future cost of discomfort, inconvenience, or pain.

An organizational or social trap is a situation in which the individual engages in behavior that has short-term advantages for the individual engaging in the behavior but immediate or long-term disadvantages for the organization or society. The classic example here is what biologist Garrett Hardin called "the tragedy of the commons."[31] A given farmer finds it to his advantage to graze an additional animal on the common pastureland. Eleven animals, though not ideal for market (but nearly so), bring a greater return than do ten animals fully ripe for market. And so, an eleventh is added. This same logic, however, is followed by each farmer; each adds an eleventh, a twelfth, a twentieth animal to the commons until its carrying capacity collapses; that is, the pastureland is unable to regenerate its grasses given such heavy use and can no longer sustain any grazing at all. At that point, Platt would say, the trap closes and all the farmers, whether they contributed to the collapse or not, suffer the loss.

In today's world (and this was Hardin's point), the water, the air, the land, the Earth's regenerative processes are the commons. And when they are contaminated—their carrying capacity diminished—all suffer. This is the tragedy of the commons. And, as both Hardin and Platt point out, the collapse or contamination occurs as a result of each individual or organization pursuing short-term gains and/or advantages (pursued because there are short-term gains and advantages to be had) only to discover that, at some point, the larger system on which they depend is no longer capable of supporting them. The short-term interests of the individual or organization collide with the current or long-term interests of the collective, to the point that all, including those who initially profited, find themselves the victim of the collapse. That is Platt's social trap: the way in which one person or group's immediate or short-term interest, if pursued far enough, can result in immediate or eventual trouble for all. Examples might include the polluting practices of some industries, the discharge of waste into public waterways, the excessive use of pesticides and fertilizers, the over-harvesting of the fishing and whaling industries, over-consumption in general, and perhaps the sole allegiance of corporations to shareholders (as opposed to the recognition that employees, communities, and the environment are shareholders of a sort as well). In addition, there is racism, classism, sexism, ageism—all the "isms" that have us respond to others not as individuals but as categories. And then there is climate change, the poisoning of the oceans, desertification. All of these constitute social and/or organizational traps in which short-term, individual focus, interest, or advantage lead to immediate or long-term collective disadvantage. Platt quotes Alexander Hamilton, who pointed out the nature of the problem in the *Federalist Papers*: "Momentary passions and immediate interests have a more active and imperious control over human conduct than general or remote considerations of policy, utility or justice."[32]

The opposite of a trap, in Platt's analysis, is a social or behavioral "fence." In these situations, short-term inconvenience or loss is traded or embraced for the sake of long-term convenience or gain. Examples of personal fences might include daily exercise, daily adherence to a healthy diet, meditation, budgeting, comparative shopping, monotonous rehearsal of a skill or technique—any activity in which the individual has to overcome his disinclination to engage in the activity en route to enjoying its longer-term benefits.

An organizational or social fence is a situation in which behavior has immediate or short-term disadvantages for the individual but immediate or long-term advantages for organization or society. Examples might include conservation practices, the removing of an obstacle that has stopped traffic (with the hope that someone will let you back in once traffic begins flowing), whistle-blowing, toll roads and bridges—in short, activities or behaviors that may be inconvenient, costly, or even dangerous for the individual who engages in them, but that have immediate or long-term benefits for the organization or larger community.

It should be noted that a fence may cease to be a fence for any number of reasons. Exercise or meditation, for example, may cease to be a fence once we find pleasure in the activity itself, not simply afterward or in the future; or, if not pleasure, then an understanding of the value of the activity so complete that we can eliminate our resistance, leaving nothing between ourselves and the practice of the activity to overcome. In other words, what starts out as a fence can cease to be a fence as the pleasure or understanding of the importance of the activity begins to align with the knowledge of its future benefits.

With Platt's concepts in mind, a restatement of the Sustainability Ethic is possible: *It is ethical to submit all personal, organizational, and environmental practices to close scrutiny, altering them until they are as sustainable and free of traps as possible. It is unethical to knowingly implement practices that ensure environmental collapse, and unethical, as well, to implement practices that diminish the health and wellbeing of individuals.*

With the Sustainability Ethic so stated, it may be helpful to look more closely at the nature of the problem being addressed. It is the problem of self-control, implied with the other ethics but brought into focus here. It is the problem of choosing between two rewards, one being offered now (that, if chosen, will lead in the long run to suffering, i.e., a trap) and one that will come in the future (that requires sacrifice now, i.e., a fence). If you are overweight and presented with the choice of eating sweets now or being thin now, you would likely have little trouble choosing.[33] If you wish to be thin, you will choose the latter. The problem occurs when you have the choice between eating sweets now and achieving your desired weight next year. With this choice, the temptation and challenge is great. It is the commons example, or nearly so, from another angle. If we are given a choice between, on the one hand, increasing our income this year by using pesticides that produce a toxic buildup in water and soil and, on the other hand, cultivation practices that are sustainable but have benefits that won't be felt for years, we will be tempted—especially if everyone else in the region is choosing the former. Or say we are presented with the choice of saving money by discharging effluents into the atmosphere or, alternatively, expending the amount required to purify emissions. Which would we choose even though we know the latter supports a clean environment and the former does not? What about the choice between exercise and television, even though we are out of shape and value a healthy body? Or the choice between the practice of our art and television, even though we value our art and have not practiced it for days or weeks? These are choice points, situations that pit the immediate against the longer term.

When an individual, organization, or industry is unable to regulate itself to the benefit of society, society may attempt to redesign the incentive/disincentive arrangements under which the individual, organization, or industry operates. To draw again from the work of Garrett Hardin: "Pipe the effluent from the polluting smokestack into the ventilation system of the Board of Director's homes and suddenly, decision-making reflects a broader, more 'environmentally-friendly' concern. Put the sewage outflow pipe upstream of the city's water intake pipe so that the city itself must contend with its waste rather than leaving it for those downstream."[34] These examples illustrate the purpose of tax incentive/disincentive programs, the establishment of superordinate regulatory authorities,[35] and full-cost or true-cost accounting systems[36] in which the social and environmental costs are added to the other costs associated with production in order to determine the price of goods. All are attempts to align the short term with the long term so that individuals and organizations pay as they go, deferring nothing in the way of cost or cleanup for others. It is government or organizational arrangements[37] with the long run in mind, interventions designed to align current decision-making with sustainable ends. And it is necessary. Individual development is such that, without arrangements of this sort, the likelihood of conduct on behalf of others—ideally all others—and on behalf of an ecologically sane and sustainable future is highly unlikely.[38]

Finally, for those individuals who embrace the requirements of the Sustainability Ethic regardless of the presence or absence of external incentives, regardless also of the inconvenience or disadvantage it brings their way, there is unique status. Their sphere of concern has become life itself and their conduct a source of inspiration for those who recognize the strength and focus such conduct requires. We cannot realize the ethical life or, ultimately, our inherent possibilities without the capacity to align present conduct with a future that is life sustaining.

"No matter what anyone tells you, when you lose business, it's almost always a relationship problem."

—James A. Autry
Love and Profit

"However valid our assessment of our enemies destructiveness may be, we merely decrease our creativity by fearing and hating them."

—John David Garcia
Creative Transformation

"Treat them all in a lofty manner lest they have cause to find thee weak."

—John Dee
Eighteenth-Century Metaphysician
Quoted in *Cosmic Trigger* by Robert Anton Wilson

Ethic 10

The Wind Harp Ethic

It is ethical to treat others as you would like to be treated even though you are not always so treated. It is unethical not to find appropriate avenues for the expression of your anger, resentment, and rage so as to keep from passing them on to, or taking them out on, others. It is unethical to engage in scapegoating.

According to the Romantic poets, there existed during the Middle Ages an instrument called the wind harp.[39] The wind harp could be affixed to a window such that wind entering the instrument from one side exited the other side as music. "We are wind harps!" exclaimed the Romantic poets, the idea being that it might be possible to so work on ourselves, so refine ourselves, that no matter what ill wind happens to be blowing, the anger, resentment, and/or rage that it produces in us is not passed on to others. Instead, it is transcended, subsumed within a larger context of understanding, not taken out on or passed on to others; the wind harp a metaphor for ending the cycle of violence. Beyond that, however, is the possibility that we might go further, the violence/violation not only not passed on to others but fully transformed; the anger, resentment and/or rage turned into acts of beauty, acts so generous or kind or full of grace that they can only be described as soulful. This is the full promise of the wind harp, a concept not unlike alchemy, the human being an instrument for turning the negative into the positive, the life negating into the life enriching.

If we follow the requirements of the Wind Harp Ethic, we do not take out our negative emotions on others, either in the moment-to-moment sense in which we pass on the abuses of everyday life to others or in the generational sense in which the violence done to one generation is passed on to the next. The wind harp concept is of enormous importance not only to the individual who embraces it—who labors to instill within herself the stillness, the equanimity, the presence of heart and mind that permits such conduct—but also to the culture that will then have siphoned from it some of its reactive, unconscious, indiscriminate anger and rage. Alice Miller, student of child-rearing practices worldwide, argued that to move the world in the direction of peace we must stop battling our parents on the battleground of our own children.[40] If you had violence and abuse visited upon you as a child, though your anger may be justified, do not visit your anger upon your own children; by this means, you will be ending a generational cycle of violence.

Take for example well-known experiments conducted during the 1960s: One of two monkeys placed in the same cage is shocked repeatedly (a mild electrical shock). Soon, the monkey that is shocked begins hitting, scratching, and otherwise abusing the other innocent, by-standing monkey. This is quite possibly the paradigm of the bully, the spouse-beater, the individual who comes home full of frustration and kicks the dog. It is one way of accounting for the rage and violence spewed in the direction of the nearest, least likely to retaliate victim—not infrequently, a loved one.

In organizations, we see the absence of the Wind Harp Ethic in the passing on of a negative mood or a negative attitude to others. The supervisor treats her employee rudely. She, in turn, treats her own employees rudely. They then treat fellow workers rudely, as the climate of the organization becomes negative overnight. Those who insist that leadership sets the tone and is therefore solely responsible for organizational morale are giving away too much. Leadership plays its role, but the Wind Harp Ethic argues implicitly that our morale is far too precious a commodity for it to be made dependent on others, even organizational leaders. The Wind Harp Ethic suggests that we are capable of being responsible for our own morale. And one of the ways we exercise this responsibility is by interrupting or even transforming a negative or destructive trend, demonstrating in the process that our morale is not fragile but is instead intact and sturdy even under difficult circumstances.

Of course, to successfully incorporate the capacity of the wind harp means that we must control our reaction to our feelings. Experience our feelings and acknowledge their legitimacy, of course. But control our reaction to them, our reaction to our anger, fear, rage, and resentment so that the blows and indifferences of life do not interfere with the behavior that in our moments of calm reflection we desire and intend. This implies control over the processing of our experience. We may not have control over the events that come our way, but we can have control over the behavior that flows from us in response to those events. It is the output and not the input that is our responsibility, and to gain control over the output means that we must master our reaction to our feelings, master it to such an extent that our feelings do not drive us to engage in behavior we regret. Philosopher John David Garcia's definition of neurosis speaks directly to this point. Neurosis,writes Garcia, is "having feelings or emotions that interfere with your ability to accomplish your purpose."[41] The Wind Harp Ethic requires that we master our reaction to our feelings to the point that the pursuit of our purpose remains intact regardless of what ill wind is blowing.

Any number of activities can prove helpful to us in our effort to control our reaction to our feelings. Exercise, meditation, gardening, the many art forms available to humans, the study of great and enduring ideas, service to others, spiritual practices of one sort or another, time spent in nature, individual and group therapies, creativity in general—all can be very helpful. Each can potentially help empty or burn off the accumulation of negative feelings; each can provide a safe and constructive way to restore balance to our perspective. Through the practice of such activities, we steady ourselves. We may even acquire a sturdiness that makes us less likely to lose track of our purpose as powerful emotions come and go. Or if, for very understandable reasons, we become disoriented and do lose track of our purpose, these activities can help us find it again with greater ease than would otherwise be the case.

Finally, to succeed even by degree with the embracing of this ethic is to benefit both ourselves and others. We spare others the indiscriminate spewing or inappropriate targeting of anger and rage, and we become less neurotic, less likely to give ourselves reason for recrimination and regret by making innocent people pay for our frustration. By this means, we give ourselves hope, esteem, optimism, as even slight success at controlling our reaction to our feelings begins to undercut the notion that we cannot be responsible for how we behave. Anger, resentment, humiliation, and rage do occur, but to not take those feelings out on others who had nothing to do with them is empowering. More empowering still is to not take those feelings out on those who *did* have something to do with them, and instead to act from reason, with forethought, compassion, the long run in mind. There is great artfulness in this, the mastery of the self. Child-rearing requires it; as does teaching. And leadership. With this ethic, the meaning of personal responsibility is expanded to include composure, equanimity, an increasing ability to not take certain events personally. Both detachment and interior peace are needed so that choice remains in play, so we can choose wisely our response rather than react robotically, though understandably, to life's affronts.

"The measure of individuals—and so of corporations—is the extent to which we struggle to complete ourselves, the energy we devote to living up to our potential."

—Max DePree
Leadership Is an Art

"No organization can be more progressive or more effective than its people."

—Henry Ford II
The Human Environment and Business

"Withdraw into yourself and look. And if you do not find yourself beautiful yet, act as does the creator of a statue that is to be made beautiful; he cuts away here, he smoothes there, he makes the line lighter, this other purer, until a lovely face has grown upon his work. So do you also: . . . never cease chiseling your statue."

—Plotinus (AD 205?–270)
Quoted in *A Guide for the Perplexed*
by E. F. Schumacher

Ethic 11

The Personal Growth Ethic

It is ethical to continue to grow as a person, to continue to increase your capacity to conduct yourself in accord with your ethics and principles. It is unethical to stop growing as a person, to not continue the lifelong process of personal/psychological growth.

It is sometimes said that one of the worst things a child can witness is the unlived life of his or her parent.[42] It is disheartening and demoralizing to see those we care about stop growing, stop expanding, settling for less in themselves than we believe they deserve. To witness this in a parent is frightening, a witnessing of the death before the death. And beyond that, there is the fear that whatever led to such a capitulation in one's parent is also in oneself.

At the same time, one of the most inspiring things a child can witness is the ongoing growth of his or her parent: to see the adaptation and adjustment that permits and reflects growth; to see discipline exercised in service to a continuing interest in life; to see curiosity, investigation, and openness. To see all of that in one's parent is to be infused with the belief that life is precious, a gift, and that despair or depression need not win out.

The Personal Growth Ethic calls on us to take responsibility for our continuing growth as persons. It asks us to pursue our full developmental potential, our inherent possibilities, suggesting that it is then that we will feel on purpose, connected with our reason for being. This ethic's admonition: grow, learn, expand awareness, refine character. Find the higher reaches of human development that give joy and perspective in the face of hardship. To do so is self-honoring, and honoring as well to those we love, as it puts before them an example that makes their conclusion that they cannot do the same less and less tenable. The opposite, of course, is to give up, settle, wait out the inevitable.

Each of us is part of a community, and within that community a part of many organizations, from family to workplace to volunteer center. To continue to grow as a person is to render ourselves increasingly relevant to the organizations of which we are a part. Personal development and social responsibility go hand in hand. As we develop, we increase our capacity to deal with the complexities of everyday life. We provide our organizations and our community with one ever-improving member, the serving of the community part and parcel with the development of the self.

Of course to grow as a person takes time. And while this may be obvious, we often behave—toward ourselves if not toward others—as if change should occur overnight. We fail to acknowledge that the changes we are attempting to bring about can be extremely difficult given that we may be contending with long-entrenched habits of thinking and doing; difficult also given the scarring that can come from childhood abuse (in any of its forms) and dysfunctional upbringings in general. Change is also extremely difficult given that there are likely to be powerful reasons for each of us to behave as we are behaving currently, incentives and disincentives locking in place the current holding pattern. To bring about desired and desirable change given these factors requires time, not to mention a certain compassionate and bemused regard for our resistance even to the change we believe good for us. Therefore, it is not weakness or a lack of belief in who and what we are to admit that we sometimes need help and should not be shy about seeking it. Therapy, in many of its forms, can be helpful, as can workshops and seminars devoted to interior development, the expansion of awareness, the cultivation and practice of mindfulness and/or meditation. Higher education of the sort that is available through great books, great teachers, the arts, the study of philosophy, the study of excellence or quality in general, the daily practice of a spiritual discipline designed to quiet the mind and/or cultivate a reverence for life—all of these can be extremely helpful. The only proviso with any of these is that they must be attempted in earnest, as even these activities can function as escapes from the difficult issues that must be addressed if growth is to be served. When attempted in earnest, however, and with the open-mindedness of Ethic 2, these forms of self-help can be pivotal, giving us at the very least perspective and perhaps the strength to maintain that perspective—one infused with kindness and a loving regard for our own halting efforts to grow as persons.

Lastly, it is by means of this ethic that we align ourselves with the biological imperative that grew us from infancy to adulthood and now, through our conscious intervening, continues our development forward to the higher levels discussed in Part I. The increasingly autonomous individual decides whether development is to continue. And as development continues, marked by the increasing capacity for ethical conduct and self-direction, there comes as well, perhaps, a reduced sense of alienation, what Owen Barfield called *cutoffness*. That, at least, would seem a possibility since continued growth as a person, according to Part I, leads to the Mature-Minded individual for whom the separation between self and other—functionally speaking—dissolves. At that level, the individual treats others as he would treat himself because the self with whom he identifies has enlarged to include them. And he treats them well, which is to say with regard for their own highest attainment, because he so likes and respects the self. This may be the height of ethical development, a state of being that makes the unethical increasingly untenable because what we are doing to others is what we are doing to ourselves.

"There is only one real deprivation, I decided this morning, and that is not to be able to give one's gift . . . The gift turned inward, unable to be given, becomes a heavy burden, even sometimes a kind of poison. It is as though the flow of life were backed up."

—May Sarton
Poet and Novelist
Quoted in *The Gift* by Lewis Hyde

"The gift is to the giver, and comes back most to him [or her]—it cannot fail . . ."

—Walt Whitman
Nineteenth-Century American Poet
From "Carol of Words"

"When man gives, 'the stream of life continues to flow. . .'"

—Gerardus Van der Leeuw
Historian and Philosopher
Quoted in *Escape From Evil* by Ernest Becker

Ethic 12

The Gift-Sharing Ethic

It is ethical to utilize your gifts, talents, and unique experience on behalf of others. Through the expression of your unique gifts, you may help others evolve and in the process acquire for yourself a greater sense of purpose and meaning. It is unethical not to share your gifts, talents, and unique experience somewhere, for the benefit of someone.

The final operating assumption of the ethics of human development is that each of us, either by virtue of birth (though that is rare) or through the living of life, acquires some insight, talent, or unique bit of experience or knowledge that is useful to others, and that may aid them in their development. We acquire a "gift." And the giving of this gift to at least one other person for their benefit is the requirement of the Gift-Sharing Ethic.[43]

Some people have acquired grand gifts, gifts and talents that require a stage from which the display of their gift brings joy, pleasure, and insight to many. Others have acquired gifts that play better one-on-one, person-to-person, parent to child, friend to friend. But whatever the nature of our gift, it is vital that we share it with at least one other person for her benefit. Philosopher/inventor Buckminster Fuller said that you can assume that you are fulfilling your purpose if you are in the process of turning your experience into products and events that bring advantage to others.[44] That is the essence of the Gift-Sharing Ethic, and the reasoning—the human logic—behind it.

Through the sharing of our gift, others (at least one other person) are benefited in whatever way is afforded by our gift (our knowledge, our insight, our creation). But as Fuller indicates, we are benefited as well. We gain a measure of fulfillment, a sense that our life, whatever the twists and turns and however wrongheaded it may have seemed at times, is nevertheless amounting to something—because here are others benefiting from what we have distilled and are able to convey. We gain a felt sense of meaning since we can point to how our life has come to something, to "this" that now we give to others for their benefit.

When consciously engaged, the parent, the teacher, the mentor is, by definition, fulfilling the requirements of this ethic. And perhaps it could be argued that this is one aspect of our evolutionary assignment: to parent, teach, and mentor one another to greater completion, greater wholeness or maturity and, in the process, gain a measure of the same for ourselves.

In our organizations and, in particular, our workplaces, there is the ongoing opportunity to accommodate the requirements of this ethic. If this does occur, the result is an enriched workplace. Individuals within the workplace are more fully aware of all that is available for solving problems and seizing opportunities. Further, any workplace that finds a way to utilize the gifts of its members necessarily enjoys the advantages of a more motivated workforce. Individuals are intrinsically motivated to share their talents, gifts, and unique strengths when they see that their gifts are valued and likely to be of benefit.

The following addition to one's job description, whatever the job, puts the spirit of this ethic front and center:

> And lastly, the individual holding this position should re-create it. He should make it new. The new version should include all that the organization found useful in the previous version while adding for the first time what is now possible given the unique talents of the new jobholder.
>
> The re-creation of this position should be done so carefully that the organization never (or only briefly) experiences the slightest decrement in overall performance.

This addition to the standard job description calls on us to engage in our work fully, drawing on and utilizing our unique gifts, whatever they are, in order to evolve the workplace and in the process, create for ourselves a greater degree of job satisfaction. At base, it announces that we are to work consciously. And that means, among other things, with an eye out for what our history and unique talents permit us to contribute.

Of course, there may be no room or interest in our organization or workplace for what we believe we can contribute beyond, simply, the doing of the job, the nature of the work or our position such that we find it impossible to add what is unique to us. But even if this is so, still we must find someone somewhere who is interested in what we have to offer and serve that person and ourselves by extending our gift.

In his book *The Gift*, Lewis Hyde wrote that gift-giving of the sort we are discussing recognizes, establishes, and maintains community.[45] The health of a community, he argues, is gauged by the amount of gift-giving occurring within it. Gift-giving, then, is a measure of the creative spirit residing in the community, a measure of its vitality, its interest in and capacity for further development, synergic development—as synergy is possible only with the flow and exchange of ideas, knowledge, and resources. The death of a group, on the other hand, is marked by the absence of the creative exchange of gifts, art, and/or knowledge.[46] Thus, gift-giving is life-giving.[47] When gift-giving occurs, individuals feel honored. They experience themselves present in the awareness of others, and so, less alienated, more able perhaps to share their own gifts. When we consciously attempt to share what is most essential to us—our truest insight, talent, or art, with sensitivity and respect, recognizing that those with whom we are sharing are deeply deserving—we fight the emptiness and even despair that can seep into the lives of those we care about, and into our own lives as well.

Finally, one last point concerning this ethic, which may extend to the ethics of human development overall: What is the most fundamental gift we ourselves have been given, the gift necessary, though not sufficient, for all other gifts? It would not be surprising if we were to conclude that time is that gift. That conclusion, coupled with the fact that this gift is of unknown and limited duration, can have a quickening effect on consciousness. For some, it is the heightened sense of time that marks the beginning of the ethical life. With no time to waste, how are we to use the time that remains? The answer, implicit throughout the discussion of the ethics of human development, is intentionally, meaningfully, to the benefit of those we care about, and, if we care enough, to the benefit of life itself. And we do this so that we may conclude that our time is well spent, used in service to what in our opinion matters most.

The fulfillment of purpose: that is what concerns us when the sense of mortality cuts to the core. Of course, we can conclude that it is too late, that too much water has passed under the bridge, and we can find ourselves wondering: "*What does it matter anyway?*" But if there is gratefulness for the time that remains, then often there will remain as well the desire to fulfill one's purpose, to take it all the way to the end, and to do so not only for the good it brings others but also so we can experience a further sense of fulfillment. The full life requires purpose, the giving of one's gift, the turning of one's experience to the advantage of others. And the human logic embedded in this line of thought, and in the Gift-Sharing Ethic itself, announces that we are benefited in return.

SUMMARY

These, then, are the ethics of human development. With them, we take responsibility for our own continuing development and, in the process, exert (indeed, must exert in order to further our development) a constructive shaping influence on others and on the organizations of which we (and they) are a part.

In the last book before his death, Buckminster Fuller wrote: "Humanity is now maintaining an unstable collection of local holding patterns, awaiting a physical or metaphysical integrity to give structure to the future and to show the way out of the darkness."[48] If by structure is meant a set of rules for guiding behavior in a direction we value, the ethics of human development offer one such structure. And we do value our own development. We value the transcending of limits, personal or otherwise, because we value the greater freedom that results. New limits also result, but in time, we value their transcending as well. The direction is toward greater freedom or wholeness, toward a growing repertoire that allows us to be at ease with ourselves in an ever-expanding circle of people, situations, and settings.

That is the final point made in this section. The ethics of human development are a means for enlarging the field of play and, along with it, our capacity to perform effectively on it. They are the rules for addressing directly the forces that establish limits (i.e., ignorance and fear), the rules for gathering the experience that leads to the transcending of those limits. Everyone is interested in a way out of the darkness, in finding the illumination that makes for greater ease of navigation, greater understanding, so that the desired difference or contribution can be made. Everyone hungers for the genuine in themselves and others. And the ethics of human development allow us to address that interest and that hunger. They are a means for assuming responsibility for our own degree of development and for assisting constructively in the development of others.

To put it another way: Each of us is issued a call to being. This call is answered with birth, but neither the call nor the need for an answer ends there. "To be or not to be" remains the question throughout our lives. And the ethics detailed here are a way of continuing to answer that question in the affirmative, a way of announcing our interest in and commitment to being, and to being more in the everyday world, where it matters so much. This is ethics as human logic, ethics as the means by which we mature and enlighten ourselves. To behave in accord with these ethics is to make more likely a future where human development, and not something less than that, is the principle value.

Part III

Dilemmas from Everyday Life

"All the world's a stage…"

—William Shakespeare, *As You Like It*

Life is a morality play. As indicated in the preface, that view suits the topic this book explores. In a morality play, actors face ethical dilemmas. They make choices. And the choices they make give the play direction and outcome while also defining the lessons that the characters in the play and we the audience are to learn.

Life is like that, at least in enough ways to make the metaphor useful. Every sphere of human endeavor—business, education, science, the fine arts, indeed, every organization of which we are a part—is a theater of sorts wherein there occurs an ongoing play. And we are actors in this play. And through our choices, we develop character while also moving the play along.

This view is helpful for several reasons. First, it emphasizes choice and the fact that through choice, we shape character (or fail to do so), and shape by degree the organizations of which we are a part. As noted previously, without the presumption of choice, the notion of ethics is out the door. Second, it announces the opportunity for the psychological/ethical growth that organizational life affords. In a sense, it is through organizations (i.e., family, school, workplace) that we grow, the ethical dilemmas faced along the way providing the opportunity for that growth. And third, it encourages us as individuals, as actors in the play, to be conscious of what we stand for, putting us in a position to spot those dilemmas, large and small, that present the opportunity for further growth.

The focus in Part III is on the moments in everyday life when conduct in accord with the ethics of human development does not come easily; that is, the moments that offer some degree of resistance. To recognize these moments, these situations or transactions for what they are, and to not let them go by as if they have no developmental importance is the first requirement. The second requirement is to address them and to do so as effectively as current abilities allow. If that results in an outcome below one's desired standard, then to learn from the experience so that the desired standard can be realized should the same or similar situations occur in the future.

SCENES FROM WORK AND LIFE

We all live lives full of challenges. Through the addressing of these challenges we make our experience, and we make ourselves. From the human logic point of view, these challenges, whether large or small, are considered ethical dilemmas, with implications for our selves and others.

These dilemmas need not be of looming importance to society. Some are, of course, but many are small matters, issues that arise between two people, within a family, or within an organization. However, all such dilemmas have certain things in common. When they occur, providing we recognize them for what they are, we can find that we experience anxiety, hesitation, even fear. We know that we are being given an opportunity, of sorts, though perhaps not a welcomed opportunity. We are being questioned in the moment about where we stand and, in an important sense, about who we are.

If we can behave in accord with our ethics and principles (or make an exception to them if an exception is warranted), then we give ourselves evidence of our strength as a person. We may also produce a beneficial difference for others. On the other hand, if we back away from the issue in question, escape and avoid, then things will remain as they are, or slide backward, while we live with a degree of self-doubt that was not there before.

Again, these dilemmas need not be of looming importance to society. For the most part, they are small matters, or seemingly so—the stuff of everyday life. But this is the stuff on which development depends: tests of creative will and of moral and ethical fortitude. Put simply, they are opportunities to display, test, and further one's integration as a person, and to do so in situations that matter.

An example of a dilemma of modest size came from the television program called *Sports Night,*[1] a situation comedy/drama focusing on the interpersonal and backstage relationships of a cast and crew putting on a nightly television sports show. In one episode, Casey McCall, one of the

Sports Night anchors, appears on the daytime talk show *The View*. The interviewer asks Casey if he selects what he wears on camera, as in the judgment of the show's panel, he looks great on camera! Casey replies that he does select his own wardrobe, a response that elicits appreciation and applause from both the panel and the audience.

This exchange seems innocent enough—except for the fact that Casey does *not* in fact select what he wears on camera. By saying that he does, he creates a dilemma for those in his workplace who know the truth of the matter.

In the next scene, Casey is in his office reviewing the tape of his performance on *The View* and feeling rather good about it. Margaret, the *Sports Night* staff member who found herself beset with what to do because of Casey's comment, knocks on his office door. Casey invites her in. After some obvious hesitation, Margaret comes to the reason for her visit. She holds up two shirts and two ties and asks Casey which tie goes best with each shirt. Casey responds by saying that the ties go equally well with both shirts. Margaret points out that one of the ties clashes with one of the shirts. She then asks which shirt would be best to wear on camera. Casey selects the shirt that, as Margaret points out, would wash out his color and make him look pale.

Margaret then asks Casey, who seems disinterested in their exchange, if he knows who selects his on-camera wardrobe. He does not. It's Joyce, she points out, one of her employees. She then asks Casey if he has any idea how much it would have meant to Joyce and her family if he had acknowledged Joyce on the air.

It is important to note that Margaret's demeanor throughout her interaction with Casey is calm and direct. She contends as effectively as she knows how with her dilemma. And though the situation is hardly of looming import to society, it is nevertheless very real. After witnessing Casey's performance on *The View*—a performance that in her opinion wronged Joyce and, in general, wronged the organization on which she, Joyce, and Casey depend—Margaret felt compelled to respond. However, the prospect of responding raised concern. Casey, if not her direct superior, is nevertheless one of the stars of the show, and as critical as anyone to the success of the program. If she handles the situation poorly, the result could be greater tension and the feeling that she has only made things worse.

Two very desirable outcomes result from Margaret's effort. First, Margaret gives herself evidence of her ability to overcome fear and act on principle, and to do so calmly, peacefully, without undue blame. She is able to walk away without regret, concluding that she has done the best she could do for herself and for the organization. Could she have given Casey her feedback more effectively? Perhaps. Some might argue that she trapped him, giving him a test that had "indirectness" in it. Still, the impression from the actual enactment of the scene is that Margaret had given considerable thought to her approach. She addressed the situation in the best way she knew how—and in so doing, she gave herself evidence of her ability to act on behalf of her own sense of right and wrong.

The second outcome was that Casey was given his own dilemma in a way that he could not dismiss. Had Margaret handled the situation less effectively, it might have been possible for Casey to conclude that she was out of line or that what she said lacked merit. He could have felt justified complaining to her superior or ignoring the issue entirely. Instead, he was left with his own internal struggle. Margaret announced by her behavior a desire to raise the standard in the organization or to make sure that a given standard prevailed. It was then up to Casey to contend with his own dilemma.

In the next scene, Casey and Dan, Casey's coanchor on the program, are broadcasting the last show of the season. They indicate toward the end of the show that they are going to depart from their normal format. Casey remarks on how some of his viewers have been commenting on how good he looks day in and day out on the show. He then acknowledges that it's Joyce who keeps both he and Dan looking so good. Dan adds that Joyce works for Margaret, who handles set design and lighting (and from what he hears, is no one to mess with).

From that point, Casey and Dan name the individuals who work behind the scenes on the program—the interns who write the cue cards, the camera operators, the people in the booth calling the shots, the director and assistant director—announcing clearly where the credit belongs.

They then announce that they will be doing more of this in the future, giving credit where credit is due.

To Casey's credit, he found a response equal to his dilemma. He responded creatively, responsibly, implicitly acknowledging his mistake and correcting it. He could have ignored the situation, including the discomfort he no doubt felt in the pit of his stomach. But to do so would have required that he shut down, separate himself from his feelings and from his sense of right and wrong. Had he done that, he would have failed to use his experience, the feedback he received from Margaret, the feelings associated with being wrong or found out, for the benefit of his own growth. He would have wasted that opportunity, setting himself up for more of the same in the future or, if not more of the same, then a certain embarrassment whenever he saw Margaret or Joyce or anyone else who knew the story.

Instead, Casey created a response of which he could be proud, one that freed him from self-recrimination while at the same time furthering an environment, a workplace, supportive of ethical and creative conduct. By his response, he announced that feedback is welcome and change is possible. A culture wherein this is broadcast by the behavior of those who are a part of it is a culture where people feel safe and hopeful—conditions that encourage creative work. Casey put a smile on the faces of his coworkers, allowing them to drop their guard, at least by degree, as he announced his interest in being a part of something better than what currently existed. He made visible to many, as Margaret had made visible to him, the standard to be upheld.

This illustrates the following point (perhaps implicit in what has preceded but worth emphasizing): The culture that surrounds us is also in us. The culture of the workplace, the culture of the school, the culture of the family—they are in us, each to varying degrees. They enter us in a variety of ways, but most substantially through the interactions we have with others, through the interpersonal give-and-take of everyday life. We are formed by this give-and-take. Our awareness comes from it, as does our capacity to adapt, solve problems, and create. And unless our desire for more awareness and more capacity is dampened or extinguished, we continue with the give-and-take, achieving perhaps new levels of psychological integration and maturity. At some point, providing we have been observant, and providing also that our culture has been supportive of our development, we realize the importance of conduct in accord with principle, of ethics, and of dilemmas of the sort just described. We see that, to a considerable degree, the integration and wholeness we achieve as individuals depends on how we choose to respond to the dilemmas and challenges that come our way. When we understand this, we obtain a new freedom. As was said previously, responsibility for further development can then fall to the self.

What follows are some additional examples of dilemmas from everyday life. Most, but not all, are from the world of work. Again, many of the situations that follow may appear small in magnitude. Still, they are likely to pose a dilemma for at least one person, and how that person responds will affect that person's development, the development of others in the situation, and, by degree, the development of the culture whether of workplace, family, or larger community.

Scene One: "The Play within the Play"

Two individuals are visiting in the hallway during a break in a staff training session.

Rex: That's what I hate about these staff training sessions.

Will: What do you mean?

Rex: I mean, tell me about my job, but spare me the rest. I'm here to do a job, not join a club. Organizational values! My values are just fine, thank you. I don't need to know about the "big picture" or whatever it is they're talking about in there!

Will: I don't know, Rex. I sort of like hearing about how this place is organized, what everybody else is doing, the stuff they think we should know.

Rex: Well, help yourself. You'll forget it in a week and you'll see then that it doesn't make any difference.

Will: You know, see how the whole thing fits together.

Rex: Do your job and collect your pay. That's how it fits together.

Will: Well what if—

Rex: It's a waste of time! We could be focusing on our own jobs, doing our own work right now. This is just stealing time. Maybe if you were the president of the company or something like that, but at our level, what does it matter?

Will: Well, it's time to go back in. The session is starting.

Rex: Time to work on my doodling!

Staff training, schooling, and education in general present dilemmas—self-forming opportunities—to all participants, especially if it is difficult to see the relevance of what is being taught. Participants can hear themselves saying privately, or to others, "Why should I have to do this? I'm an adult! I don't need to hear about organizational values or teamwork or whatever it is they're talking about! It's a waste of time!"

It should be pointed out that the scenes presented in Part III are, for the most part, without context. For example, in this scene we do not know the history of staff training in this organization or the history of the individuals involved. There could be some truth to what Rex is saying. He may have found little value in previous staff training sessions. Still, staff training is a self-making moment for all who attend because it puts the concepts of choice and attitude front and center. It is the play within the play, an opportunity to exhibit and exercise the attitude we bring to work, school, or even life. This is so even if the content of the training seems irrelevant or if the material is poorly presented. There is always the opportunity in such sessions to interact, to ask questions, to shape the training experience in a direction that is more meaningful. To check out or retreat into doodling is to exercise the wrong muscles. We strengthen neither attitude nor creativity in that way. If the material is relevant but already known, there is the opportunity to assist others in their understanding. We make our organizations stronger to the extent that we pitch in, ensuring that relevant information is understood and the willingness to help others is modeled.

"All right, fine," you say. "I'll attend the session, but I'm not going to contribute. I'll do the absolute minimum and work on other things if I can." Or perhaps your response is something like, "I'm going to take issue with everything: the trainer, the material, the timing of the breaks, you name it. This is ridiculous and I'm not going to sit by and have my time wasted." To varying degrees, these responses occur in all of us. We have all been the person with arms folded, wearing a perpetual frown, looking for mistakes, whispering discontent to those around us. That person is in each of us—or can be—and we must get very good at detecting the moment that person shows up in us. Detect and self-correct, with compassion but little patience, for this attitude serves only to harm ourselves and to harm the organization overall. It is a violation of several ethics at once, if not all of them.

When Rex adopts this stance, he presents Will with a dilemma. Will, who seems to embrace the training event for what it might bring, is left with the choice of what to do. Whether he will do all that he knows to do or should expect of himself will be up to him to decide. He does offer Rex reasons for why the training might be of value. And he remains true to his own view, not going over to Rex's side when others might have been tempted to do so. Maybe he thinks the way Rex is behaving is not worth the bother—Rex just being Rex—and that in the course of things, it won't matter much. On the other hand, if the content of the training is important, if how one approaches such events is important (affecting, for example, the training experience for others), then what Rex is choosing to do is harming the organization. Maybe Will feels he has done all that is reasonable. The issue doesn't warrant more, and if it really is important, it's an issue for Rex's supervisor, not a colleague or teammate. But if Will cares about the organization and cares about Rex, he may wonder if he could do more, whether he might find a thoughtful, assertive, or humorous way of calling Rex to the approach that would make the team stronger—the playful or serious nudging that says: Let's do this and get what we can from it. Of course, this would have to be done skillfully, born of a desire to create and be a part of an organization worthy of its members—with members who, in turn, insist that they and their colleagues are worthy of the organization.

Scene Two: "Making Work for Others"

Two individuals within an organization are finishing a job and are anxious to go home. This scene could occur in a school, a university, a corporation, a studio, a ranch, a construction site, or any number of other locations.

Jake: Well, Mike, does that do it?

Mike: That does it. And about time, wouldn't you say?

Jake: Absolutely!

Mike: Come on, let's get outta here.

Jake: I'm with you, just as soon as I put this equipment away and tidy up a bit.

Mike: Are you kidding? I've come in plenty of times and found this place in worse condition than this.

Jake: It'll only take a minute. Besides, I've seen the morning schedule. It's pretty tight.

Mike: Look, I wasn't hired to clean this place up. Let's go. They'll deal with it in the morning. We could be thirty minutes putting this stuff away.

Jake: Yeah, but they could be put out at us for leaving this.

Mike: They'll get over it. Chances are it will all be forgotten by the time we get in tomorrow. Nobody will say anything. You'll see. Now let's go!

Ethic 1, Corollary 4 states that it is unethical to make work unnecessarily harder for others. And that is exactly what could happen here if Mike has his way. Further, if Mike is correct, this same thing has happened in the past (i.e., "I've come in plenty of times and found this place in worse condition than this"). With Mike's decision to leave, Jake is confronted with a dilemma. What he chooses to do will have implications for himself and others in the organization. If he goes along with Mike, knowing that he is making work for others, then he is likely to think less of himself.

His self-respect will be diminished, at least by degree, knowing that he has given in to expedience or social pressure at the expense of others or at the expense of his values.

This is to say nothing of the impact such a decision is likely to have on others in the organization. Maybe, as Mike says, nothing will come of it. But even if nothing is said, such actions can breed resentments that are likely to surface if similar situations occur again. And how can they not occur? If Jake goes along with Mike, then he has weakened himself, however slightly. By failing to exercise his capacity to stand up for what he believes in, he has rendered himself less ready for similar situations in the future. Unless his disappointment with himself forces a reversal of mind or unless someone confronts him, more of the same can now be expected from both Jake and Mike.

Is there nothing that Jake can do or say to turn the moment in the direction of his values, his ethics? Is he too tired, weak, or forgetful to act on his own behalf? Is Mike's approval more important to him than his allegiance to himself, his family, and the organization on which he and his family depends? Or does he simply not see the moment for what it is until later, when someone complains? Whatever the case, Jake has these questions to consider. Providing that he permits the self-examination these questions invite, he will be the better for it, perhaps resolving to do differently next time. And if he does do differently next time, he will have used his experience to the benefit of himself and others. On the other hand, if he avoids the self-review, avoids the resolution to do differently next time, avoids even raising a question concerning end-of-shift responsibilities, then it is hard to imagine that he is making anything but trouble for himself and others in the near term. Whatever Jake chooses, however, it is worth emphasizing that it is here, in situations so seemingly small, that the opportunity for self-making occurs (a theme to which we will return in Part V). Here, also—in situations of no greater magnitude than what Jake and Mike are experiencing—is where the culture of the organization is felt and, depending on the choices made, either furthered along or gradually undone.

Scene Three: "The Creative Culture"

Two coworkers come across one another in the hall, in the lunchroom, in the elevator, etc.

Jane: Hey, Carl, I've been thinking about you. What's going on?

Carl: Nothing much. Same old routine, really. What's going on with you?

Jane: Everything's just great! Say, Carl, whatever happened to that idea of yours?

Carl: What idea is that?

Jane: You know, the one about scheduling.

Carl: Forget it.

Jane: Forget it? What do you mean? You were all fired up about it a week ago.

Carl: Yeah, well, they really know how to put out the fire around here.

Jane: You mean they shot it down?

Carl: I mentioned it, figuring they'd go for it . . . All they wanted was facts and figures. Turned the whole thing into a huge obstacle.

Jane: Well, that's not so surprising, is it? I mean it was a pretty basic change you were proposing. Maybe they just wanted to make sure that everything was covered.

Carl: Look, this place is afraid of anything and everything that is out of the usual. I think the idea scared them. I learned my lesson.

Jane: Your lesson?

Carl: I'm saving my ideas for after work. This place will never change.

Jane: Yeah, I know what you mean. They say they want your ideas, but as soon as you come up with one—

Carl: They get a big frown on their face.

Jane: Anyway, where are you off to now, Carl?

Carl: Well, believe it or not, I'm attending staff development's workshop on creativity.

Jane: You're kidding!

Carl: I'm not kidding. But don't worry. I'm one guy who knows the score.

In this scene, Jane is met with a dilemma. At first she stands up for the possibility that the requests made by Carl's superiors when he presented his idea were reasonable and that they may be thinking of potential implications of which Carl is not aware. Perhaps they simply want to ensure the likely success of the proposed idea. From their point of view, she suggests, Carl's idea may be an "idea fragment" that must be elaborated upon before they can take it seriously, the mere fact that they have asked for elaboration a sign that the idea has promise.

It is true that we don't know what has happened to Carl (or perhaps to others that Carl knows) when ideas have been presented in the past. Maybe they have been good ideas, or maybe they haven't—that, too, is possible. Maybe his ideas have been shot down or put aside before. Or maybe they have simply fallen on deaf ears time and time again. Whatever the case may be, Carl apparently believes that he cannot contribute to the organization as he would like, that his creative ideas for improvement are not welcome. This raises a pivotal dilemma for Carl. Is the organization worthy of the life he wants to give it? Does he have the time and energy apart from his other tasks to follow up on his ideas for change? And if not, can he remain a member of the organization without losing his commitment to it? If he must leave, can he do so without damage, without the burning of bridges, finding in the process an organization in which he can contribute in the way he would like?

In the beginning of the scene, Jane encourages Carl to extend the benefit of the doubt. But as Carl continues with his indictment,

Jane joins in and, in so doing, gives support to Carl's disgruntlement. The Organizational Ethic, Corollary 8 states: "It is ethical to create organizational improvements, unethical not to help the organization evolve." This is based on the notion that organizations grow, evolve, and remain relevant through creative work—that creative work gives life to the organization. But it is based also on the notion that individuals grow and evolve through their effort to work creatively, to formulate and implement creative change. This is what Jane's dilemma is about. Initially, she supports a culture of personal responsibility, of personal growth in which neither Carl nor his superiors are assumed to be incompetent or wrong, in which more creative work may be all that is needed on Carl's part. She then changes her position and falls in league with Carl, creating in the process a subculture in which cynicism and blaming prevail.

This change in Jane's position raises for her an issue worth considering, if she can see it. Why, she might ask herself, did she change her allegiance in the middle of this exchange? We do not know Jane's history with Carl or with the organization any more than we know Carl's. Nor do we know the history or character of the organization. But what good does Jane do Carl or the organization by supporting Carl in his withdrawal? She only avoids her own challenge, failing herself as she fails to say to Carl (in whatever way she finds best) that no one is keeping him from being creative; that even here he can continue to create, and, if not here, then elsewhere. And in any event, he should remember that what he is ultimately creating (whatever his work might be) is the upkeep of his own morale, which is certain to diminish if he does not behave in ways that nourish it.

Ultimately, the dilemma that confronts both Carl and Jane has to do with the victimization of the self. Instead of finding a way to create the change they desire; or accepting the fact that the desired change cannot be created now given their time, energy, and the organization as it stands; or creating a way to leave because that is the self-honoring thing to do, Carl and Jane complain. And by complaining, which leads not to action but only to more complaining, they make victims of themselves. At some level, they cannot help but be depressed about the option they have selected. Instead of exercising their power to create, they slip into anger—anger at themselves (though this might be unconscious) and at the organization. In the sharing of their disgruntlement, they form a small culture not of growth but of commiseration, a situation in which the feedback and support they provide one another keeps them oblivious to the harm they are doing to themselves and the organization.

Ethic 11 states: *"It is ethical to continue to grow as a person, to engage in those activities that support and are likely to result in psychological/ethical development, unethical to stop growing as a person, to settle for less than we deserve and are capable of becoming."* This is the ethic in question for Carl and Jane, the ethic in question with all the dilemmas presented in Part III. How we choose to interact in these situations provides us with the information we use to assemble our self-understanding, our self-knowledge—the information we use to define ourselves. This is why ethical dilemmas even of the size we are describing are so important. Like the individuals in the previous scenes, Carl and Jane are engaging in self-defining behavior, driving home (albeit perhaps subliminally) their conclusion concerning the stuff of which they are made. By what they choose to do, they are building and reinforcing a self-concept—as are we all. Through interactions with ethical dilemmas, small and relatively minor though they may seem, the self is made (or the self-concept is made), and with it the sense of who and what one is and, also, the sense of what one might become given the influence and potential control individuals have over their own making.

Scene Four: "Feedback and the Observing Self"

Two people are discussing a meeting that has just ended. They are peers within a large organization.

Alicia: Well, frankly, I think I said exactly what I needed to say.

Harold: Well, it's just that—

Alicia: Look, if it's junk, it's junk. Why should I pamper him?

Harold: I know, but we need everyone—

Alicia: All I said was that his idea had been tried before and that we all had to do better than that. And that's the truth.

Harold: Alicia, I was there. He hadn't even finished before you were shuffling through papers, raising your eyebrows, cutting him off. You wouldn't like it if it had been the other way around.

Alicia: You know what he was proposing. We tried that same idea two years ago, and it didn't work then. Now why should I pretend that—

Harold: I'm not talking about the idea. I guess I'm talking about the climate.

Alicia: The climate! Now you've lost me. If people are so thin-skinned that a little reality shuts them down, then they're in the wrong business.

Harold: Well, I think it makes a difference. If you—

Alicia: We're in a race, you know? And I want the most from my people.

Harold: That's what I'm talking about. It's just that—

Alicia: [Sounding defensive.] Oh, I get it. You know how to work with people and I don't, is that it?

Harold: No, no, no. It's not that at all. It's just that sometimes you can get more if—

Alicia: Well, I think I've done just fine, thank you. But if you want to tell me how I should act . . .

Harold: Look, I didn't mean to overstep. I was only trying to help. Maybe I should have—

Alicia: See, I work with a certain kind of person. Our side of the business is a little more complicated than yours. It's a little faster and draws a more ambitious kind of person. I don't think you've ever worked in my area before, have you?

Harold finds himself in a pickle. His dilemma comes courtesy of Alicia, who is feeling increasingly defensive and angry about Harold's attempt to discuss her handling of a subordinate. Everything Harold attempts to say gets cut off and seems only to lead to more resentment on Alicia's part. Is there anything Harold can do to turn this around? He has a challenge.

Can he keep himself from becoming angry? That is perhaps the first test. Can he view the exchange impersonally even though Alicia feels so backed against the wall that she is making it personal? Can he create space for Alicia to expel her emotions, and then continue in a way that allows his personal regard for Alicia to come through? Or must he excuse himself and come back to the discussion later, when things have cooled down, pursuing his point of view and listening again to hers?

All of this depends on what Harold has made of himself as a person. Leaving the situation where it is, however, is to leave it unresolved. And unresolved issues between people fester, usually for both parties but certainly for the one who is sensitive to the price he is paying. At the very least, the individual (Harold in this case, but perhaps Alicia as well) experiences an increase in self-chatter, repeatedly reliving what was said and what he wished he would have said instead. Considerable mental energy gets devoted to unresolved issues. And perhaps this is what must happen if the readiness to deal with the same issue or person in question is to grow. But throughout the period during which the issue remains unresolved, the individual finds he is becoming all the more aware of the importance of dealing effectively with people as issues arise, and if not then, soon thereafter. The cost of not doing so—to one's own equanimity, if nothing else—is simply too high. Increasingly, individuals find themselves desiring and seeking to operate with an expanded perspective, a perspective that is increasingly rational, laced with compassion and humor so that there exists the necessary sturdiness and objectivity to see and not get caught in the drama of the moment.

In this example, Alicia has lost it (or, perhaps, has yet to *acquire* it—again, we have no knowledge of Alicia or Harold prior to this scene). The "it" is her perspective, or—to put it another way—her objectivity, her ability to separate herself from her performance. Without "distance" from her performance, Alicia experiences Harold's critique as a critique of what she considers herself to be, and not of a performance that she can view objectively.

Alicia's challenge is the challenge we all face: namely, to evolve a commitment to our own growth to such an extent that we can hear and even welcome feedback on anything, feedback that we can then assess for its usefulness no matter how uncomfortable it makes us. If there is truth in the feedback we receive, even if it is delivered poorly, we act on it; we experiment with corrective action. If there is no truth in the feedback, we do not act on it, but we do not dismiss it, either. Nor do we insulate ourselves from the prospect of receiving further feedback. The task is to remain open, as dictated by Ethics 2 and 4. In the language of the previous paragraph, Alicia is unable to keep herself open because she perhaps identifies too strongly with her performance. She responds defensively because she thinks of her performance as a part of who she is rather than an expression of who she is. If Alicia can shift some of her identity away from her performance and see herself rather as the coordinator of that performance, then the more mutable her performance will become, something she *does* rather than something she *is*. As a consequence, she will be able to view her performance more objectively, with less bias and self-protection in the equation.

Thus far throughout this book, the self has been referred to but not defined.[2] At this point, it might be useful to introduce two definitions, as there is value in recognizing that we are at least two selves throughout our lives, or one self with two aspects: the observing self[3] and the created self.

The observing self is the awareness that develops in us very early in life, an awareness that looks out through our eyes and allows us to see the world from our point of view. This awareness develops gradually as the result of a thousand interactions and untold coaxing, through nurture and language. Eventually, however, it is there: an awareness of self, a capacity to "see" ourselves in the world, watching as we walk off to elementary school, learn to ride a bike or drive a car—a capacity to witness ourselves. The observing self is sometimes considered the first self, the core self,[4] providing a locus point to which experience is connected throughout a lifetime, making possible a continuity of consciousness. It is the observing self that we refer to when we say that we feel we are the same as we have always been—the same person, the same age, in a sense, timeless.[5]

The created self, on the other hand, is the self that can be observed, the self that is witnessed by both the observing self *and* by others. It is the self that operates in the world and that possesses a multifaceted repertoire that grows as the years go by, a repertoire shaped by the environment and, increasingly (if we are fortunate), by choice. It is the created self to whom we refer when we say "I am that"—meaning, for example, I am a father, a brother, a blue-collar worker, a baseball player, a man of many interests, or whatever the case may be. We are that, though "that" is ever changing, not the same today as yesterday and different again tomorrow.

In so saying, we are partially correct: Yes, we are that, the created self, the ever-changing outcome of all our interactions. But we are also the observing self, a seemingly timeless and unchanging awareness with our point of view. We are two selves: the one that behaves or performs and the one that observes, the work of art (or the "piece of work"!) and the witness.

Over the course of a lifetime, it is important that we remain connected to both aspects of the self, as each is critical to the other and to our own sense of wholeness. The problem, however, is that from time to time, the emphasis placed by the outer world on the created self, the self that must behave, that must perform, is so great that we lose track of the observing self. We come to identify entirely with the created self. This may be understandable, even natural in a sense, but there is a price to pay. The created self is on the side of becoming, on the side of fitting in or standing out. It is about consuming, creating, destroying, about the living of life across a lifetime of goals, disappointments, victories, and apprehensions. It is about the drama of everyday life. To identify with the created self is understandable, but to identify with it too strongly is to become partially unconscious, leaving behind the capacity to watch the drama without being pulled into it. The created self is on the side of becoming, while the observing self is on the side of being, and we are both at once. To identify too strongly with the created self is to lose perspective.[6]

This is not to say that we do not or should not, at times, become fully absorbed in what we are doing, wrapped up in it entirely. There is joy in that, and perhaps necessity. Excellence in performance may require it. But we should not lose sight of the fact that we are more than that, always able to step back and gain the perspective of the observing self, that aspect of ourselves that permits a degree of objectivity not available in the throes of an emergency or in the burst of creative expression.

To put it another way, the observing self "sees," and in seeing, permits us to experience ourselves as more than what is seen. If we are the roles we adopt, the stream of thoughts and emotions that emerge in us, the actions that flow from us—indeed, if we are all that constitutes the created self—we are also something more. For all these actions, emotions, thoughts, and beliefs can be observed. They are "objects" of a subject capable of witnessing them. To experience the witnessing as well as the becoming can help to undercut the seriousness and sense of high stakes that is sometimes associated with the created self, since that self is not felt to be the end-all of who we are. The observing self provides perspective, a point of view that we acquire early in life, that is ours alone and that feels timeless. It is awareness of self and of life; and whenever that awareness is present, we experience ourselves as more than the time-bound roles we have adopted.

There is a presumption here, or perhaps a hypothesis: To identify completely with the role we are playing—whether that role is father, actor, singer, teacher, what have you—to identify completely with the created self, is to become slightly unconscious. And in the end, this damages our ability to fully embody and creatively express the requirements of that role. It leads to a "robotizing," a loss of suppleness and grace. It takes the play out of the role and leads to clumsiness in the face of the more nuanced and subtle requirements of whatever role we are in. In other words, to become unconscious in this way is to lose the opportunity for mastery, mastery of whatever role we wish to play and, eventually, mastery of the self. It is to lose the capacity for detachment within involvement,[7] a capacity—according to philosopher Bruce Wilshire—necessary for and characteristic of all art, including the art of life.

All of this brings us back to Harold and Alicia and the dilemma that each faces (and that we all face), namely: whether or not we can accept the feedback we are receiving, accept it so that the feedback (however it is delivered) can be evaluated and acted upon if improvements or benefits are to be had. Or, are we so identified with the behavior that is the focus of the feedback (feedback that is perhaps delivered poorly and in an emotionally charged situation) that in order to maintain our equilibrium, we find we must dismiss the feedback, avoid it, escape from it—anything to keep in place our current sense of self? The focus here is not on feedback that might be acceptable to us, feedback on how to improve a specific skill we have already decided we wish to improve. Here the focus is on feedback that deals with our wrongheadedness, with the ways in which we are unconscious and our own worst enemy; feedback about our false identifications, about our total attachment to ways of behaving that are destructive of oneself and others; feedback that is personal and difficult to hear but crucial to our development as persons. This feedback needs to be delivered sensitively and thoughtfully. But however it is delivered, it must be heard and responded to constructively, creatively, and sooner rather than later. And this requires presence of mind, the ability to step back into the role of witness[8]—in other words, the presence of an observing self.

Alicia stands in for all of us on this issue, as does Harold in a slightly different way. Each is being tested on their commitment to feedback, but tested also on their sense of themselves, on their knowledge of who they consider themselves to be. When we mistreat others, it is understandable and almost automatic for the person we have mistreated to ask: "Who do you think you are?" It is an excellent question, for it just may be that much of the mistreatment we deliver to ourselves and others is due to the fact that we are confused about who we are. We have lost perspective. We are not merely the role we are playing. We are that and more, both created self and observing self. And our inability to experience this fact (as the observing self permits) allows the passions of the moment to overtake us. We become, in those moments, less conscious, smaller than we really are. This is critical because often the feedback we receive is not only about the lack of skill or effectiveness in our conduct, but about the way in which we are confused, unconscious, robotic, or impersonal—about our failure to be as large or as purposeful or as conscious as we otherwise might be. This feedback is about our enlightenment, where we exhibit it and where we do not, and it is the most important feedback we ever receive.

Scene Five: "Choice and Awareness"

A group of managers is meeting with the head of their division, who is speaking with fervor and alarm.

Harry: They're giving me all kinds of grief! I'm talking about the other division heads. It sounds like they're kidding, but it's more than that. They're talking about how we're behind on what we promised, about how we're not going to make our quota. They know it's not our fault entirely, but they're serious. I hate going to those meetings. Puts me in a bad position. I know what to say, don't get me wrong. Still, past all that kidding, they're saying that we're not holding up our end! I know they're concerned. I'm concerned. It's not good . . .

Harry's remarks continue, characterized by concern, resentment, and a touch of anger. The managers listen intently—all except Ben who, though listening, is also witnessing his decision to not get involved. He stops himself from asking what is usually on the tip of his tongue; namely, How can we solve this problem? How can we make this situation better? By that decision, that choice, Ben removes himself from the problem and, by degree, from the organization.

Ben's stance may change. If the problem worsens, he may choose to get involved. But if not, if he instead chooses to stop himself again and again from (in effect) asking how the problem (and perhaps other problems as they arise) might be solved, he will remove himself even further from the organization. Taken to the extreme, if Ben continues on this course, he is likely to be confronted. His supervisor, his workmates, tired of his lack of involvement, will call on him to shape up. And if they have tried that but to no avail, then they may ask him to leave. The irony is that if Ben is unwilling to acknowledge the way in which his own choices have removed him from the organization, he might exclaim, "How dare they! How dare they ask me to leave!" when in truth, Ben had been choosing not to be there for some time.

This is potentially a great moment in Ben's life, a turning point. If, upon reflection, Ben is able to assume responsibility for the loss of his job, then he will take a meaningful step in the direction of his own agency as a person, and a step away from his view of himself as a victim. This is his challenge: To recognize that we sometimes "do it to ourselves," that we sometimes create or participate in creating the negative events that come our way. Out of ignorance, fear, fatigue, or a lack of self-regard we make choices that are self-destructive. It is the ill-advised person, therefore, who does not reflect on how he may have participated in producing the unhappy circumstances that surround him. Whatever Ben does with his experience, whatever he concludes, it is worth considering that his situation mirrors what many of us do to ourselves more often than we may want to acknowledge.

Consider, for example, how relationships sometimes end. Alice announces to Ted that their relationship is not working, perhaps has not been working for some time. Ted responds by saying: "It's not my fault! What about you?" but does not choose to ask—in fact, consciously stops himself from asking—"How can we make this better?" Alice complains that she cannot go on like this, perhaps even proposes corrective measures. This goes on for months, even years. Still, Ted chooses not to address the issue, preferring argument or withdrawal. Eventually, Alice asks Ted to leave when, in a very meaningful sense, Ted left long ago. Again, as with Ben, if choices are not acknowledged, if there is the pretense that choice is not involved, then Ted may scream, "How dare she! She is responsible for this disaster, not me!" when, in fact, Ted played his part and more in creating the outcome.

Whether in the workplace or in private life, this is the Free Choice Ethic calling on us to live a life wherein, increasingly, we take responsibility for the success of our involvements and for the quality of our experience. The above examples have been stripped of the complexity that necessarily accompanies the ending of a relationship, whether with one's workplace or in one's personal life. But the core of the issue comes down to the choices we make, choices that may go by quickly but that leave their mark.

The outcome that befalls Ben is largely, perhaps entirely, self-caused. He chooses to not be involved. Though he comes to work each day, from the organization's point of view, he is rarely there! Does Ben want to leave the organization? Does Ted want to leave the relationship? Were both without the courage or conviction to own up to what they were choosing, so much so that they were willing to make someone else act on behalf of what they themselves actually wanted? Did they even know what they wanted? Were they unaware of what they were doing? This is a hard line of inquiry, but it is the inquiry required by the Free Choice Ethic, the purpose of which is to push awareness down into the fine grain of give-and-take between self and world, to make fully conscious and one's own what was previously unconscious or perhaps denied. This can be a very difficult, even painful process, a process of excavation and reconstruction as hardened habits and destructive tendencies are unearthed and examined, their hold over us wrestled free as we will ourselves more often in the direction of our values and purpose. Freedom and responsibility are expanded in this way.

"Which ship goes oftenest on the rocks or to the bottom?" asks Don Juan rhetorically in George Bernard Shaw's play "Don Juan in Hell." "The drifting ship or the ship with a pilot on board?"[9] The answer, of course, is that the drifting ship goes oftenest on the rocks. Drifting or otherwise refusing to take responsibility for where we are heading permits past conditioning, the will of others, larger and perhaps indifferent forces to determine direction and outcome. With a pilot—an increasingly conscious and responsible pilot—principles and current values can have their say.

Unless Bill and Ted recognize and take responsibility for the choices they are making, unless they in fact stop denying that choice is involved, then they will prove themselves hard cases, questionable learners, and they will wind up in one situation after another of the sort described.

On the other hand, if Ben and Ted can step back far enough to witness their own involvement in creating their unhappy circumstances, then they will substantially expand their awareness and hopefully gain a degree of responsibility they did not have before.

There are victims in this world; there's no denying that. We are not always, by any means, choosing or helping to create the outcomes that befall us. The above analysis is simply an effort to examine our own role, if any, in creating the "victimhood" we believe we experience. Certainly, the will of others and forces beyond our control have their say. And at any given moment, these other factors can affect our lives dramatically; affect for example the organizations and relationships of which we are a part, even whether or not our involvement is possible. But if it is possible, then the Free Choice Ethic offers a cautionary note—and a hopeful one, as well. It states that with respect to the organizations and relationships of which we are a part, we are involved by choice. No one is forcing us to be involved. We are choosing to be involved, or choosing not to be involved, as the case may be. And by our choices, our decision-making and follow-through, we participate in the creation of our experience. Yes, there are many factors at play, from the personal to the societal, but the Free Choice Ethic insists that we nevertheless impose a high standard on ourselves: We have choice, and to an extent greater than we sometimes acknowledge, we craft and compose our lives. That is the view the Free Choice Ethic encourages us to embrace. By adherence to this view, we test and perhaps expand our ability to create. At the very least, we decrease the likelihood that we will conclude that we have been victimized by others when, upon close examination, we see that in some instances, quite possibly, we made choices that contributed to the undesirable situation in which we find ourselves.

Scene Six: "The Wind Harp"

This script has five sections. Each section could occur over the course of a day or in rather rapid sequence. Each is between a supervisor and a supervisee.

Section 1:

Alex: Good morning, Lois. How are you this fine morning?

Lois: Just great! How are you, Alex?

Alex: Great! Say, Lois, if you've got a minute, I'd like to share with you what we've come up with as a solution to that scheduling problem we discussed the other day.

Lois: Sure, Alex. I'd love to. Let me talk to Chris first, and then I'll be right with you.

Section 2:

Lois: Hi, Chris. Are you available?

Chris: Available for what, Lois?

Lois: To go over the revisions to our policies and procedures manual. I've drafted the changes and we had talked about discussing them first thing this morning.

Chris: Oh, right. Yes, I do want to go over them. I'm looking forward to it. Let me get with James for about five minutes and then we'll do it. And thanks in advance, Lois, for your work on this.

Section 3:

Chris: Good morning, James. How are you?

James: Come in and have a seat, Chris. Close the door if you would.

Chris: Sure. What's up?

James: I don't know what it's going to take, Chris. The performance of your department has been a disappointment to me. I'm wondering if the responsibility is too much, if maybe we ought to think about rearranging things.

Chris: James, I don't understand. I thought everything was fine. You've never mentioned anything before.

James: I'm very concerned at this point.

Chris: Well, no, uh, yes, we'll work it out . . . whatever it takes. I had no idea. What can I do?

James: I'm going to give that some thought. Right now, I'm late for a meeting. We'll meet later today or sometime tomorrow and figure out the best course of action.

Section 4:

Lois: Hi, Chris. Back from your meeting with James?

Chris: Yep.

Lois: OK. Well, here are the revisions. Pretty well done, if I do say so myself. As you can see—

Chris: Did I say I was ready to do this?

Lois: Well, no. I just thought that when you got back, we were going to—

Chris: Well, you thought wrong. Why don't you use a little common courtesy and ask me if I'm ready to deal with this stuff? It's not exactly the most exciting reading we're talking about here.

Lois: I know. I didn't say it was. I just thought—

Chris: Look, Lois, I'll call you when I'm ready.

Section 5:

Alex: Just the person I was looking for. All set?

Lois: All set for what?

Alex: For the scheduling solution we came up with. I think you're going to like it.

Lois: Alex, to tell you the truth, going over the scheduling issue is just about the last thing I want to do right now.

Alex: Oh, I just thought—

Lois: When the time is right, we'll deal with it. Understand?! And right now is not the time.

Alex: Of course. It's just that—

Lois: Look, Alex, use some judgment, would you?

The Wind Harp Ethic states that it is ethical to treat others as you would like to be treated even though you are not always so treated yourself; unethical not to find appropriate and safe avenues for the release of your anger, resentment, or rage. In sections 4 and 5 of this script, this is precisely the opposite of what appears to be happening. Chris takes the anger and resentment created by the way he was treated by James and turns it on Lois, who, in turn, takes her anger and resentment out on Alex. And poor Alex—what does he do? Well, it depends. If he is as reactive as Chris and Lois, he may kick the dog, verbally abuse his wife and children, or worse. As indicated in the discussion of the Wind Harp Ethic, this is the classic way in which organizational cultures (whether of the workplace or the family) become negative overnight; the way in which more anger is accumulated than can be managed or released safely.

And why? Concerning this example, the focus could be on the primitive management style exhibited by James. His willingness to raise a performance issue with Chris when there was no time for discussion is hardly enlightened leadership, though it does occur. The issue to be focused on here, however, is what Chris chooses to do with the feelings and emotions that arise in response to this treatment by James. Does he hold on to them, to be worked with and processed as he readies himself for a later discussion with James? Or does he allow them to overtake him, influencing how he will behave toward the next person in line? He does the latter. And then Lois—the next person in line—does the same with Alex. Was there nothing else either of them could have done? Was

Chris incapable of pausing for a moment, collecting his thoughts, perhaps letting Lois know that he had just been in a difficult meeting and now needed to spend his time differently? The same could be asked of Lois. We could also ask both Lois and Alex (and perhaps Chris): Was there no way for you to ask the person who was treating you rudely, "Is there something wrong? Is there something I can do?" or perhaps even, "If it's me, I know we can work it out. If it's not me, then maybe I can help." Is this too much to ask of us in the midst of interactions of this sort? Beyond that, whatever Chris, Lois, or Alex might have said—and in this script, they said nothing to change things—they nevertheless had the option of not passing their anger and resentment on to the next person in line.

Our inability to behave in accord with the Wind Harp Ethic is the way in which we participate in, rather than interrupt, the spirit killing that goes on in families, organizations, and society in general. It is the way in which we damage, at least potentially, the morale, confidence, self-esteem, and drive of others. Rather than putting a stop to the violence and abuse, we join in, spreading the damage done to us on to others. On the other hand, when we do not participate in this cycle of abuse, when we do not pass on to others the damage done to us, we perform a very important service. We leave others untouched by the negative and perhaps touched by the positive, moving them to consider that it is possible to remain conscious and purposeful even when offended or hurt.

In the above example, several individuals failed to stop themselves from passing their anger and resentment on to others. They were mistreated, but they did not address the mistreatment either in the moment or later, after having kept it to themselves. Instead, they passed the mistreatment on. The result, when they think about it—and they will think about it eventually—is that they will think less of themselves, and both their morale and the morale of the organization or family will be diminished.

The dilemma depicted here invites us to learn to manage our feelings, to not allow our negative feelings, however they have arisen, to drive us to conduct we regret. At a deeper level, however, this dilemma invites us to enlarge our perspective, to expand it to the point that we do not take such experiences personally; a perspective that allows us right then and there to recognize that the behavior of the other person is not so much about us as it is about a frustration or a fear the other person cannot contain. To not take things personally, to not respond in such situations as though a personal affront has occurred, is an achievement of a high order. It necessarily implies the observing self, detachment within involvement, but it does not mean that we do not respond. It means that the full range of possible responses remains in play, our range of motion, our flexibility, our full repertoire not limited by our anger or resentment but, rather, available so that we can match the best and wisest that is in us to the requirements of a difficult situation.

Scene Seven: "Where Is Me?"

Here the scene shifts from the workplace to a busy downtown street. A homeless man approaches a passerby.

Homeless man: Do you have any change? I sure could use it if you've got it to spare!

This event is a common occurrence in many locales. It is an event about which many people have very strong feelings. There are too many variables at play to say exactly how one should respond. Homelessness, especially street homelessness, can be associated with drug and alcohol addiction, mental illness, or domestic violence. There is a lack of employment in many communities, as well as a lack of affordable housing. At the same time, there are food banks, emergency shelters, housing facilities, and charities to which one can give in an effort to address the problem. It's not clear at all how one should address this situation. An assessment in the very moment it occurs is required.

If there is aggression in the request, that is one thing; if there is not (as is presumed here), it is quite another. Someone wants something from us. We may or may not have it to give, and even if we do have it to give, we may not want to give it for any number of legitimate reasons.

In Zora Neale Hurston's novel *Their Eyes Were Watching God*, there is a passage pertinent to the scene above.[10] Hurston tells the story of Janie, a black woman coming of age during the 1920s and 1930s in Florida and Georgia. In her effort to recount her life, Janie tells a friend that she hardly knows where to begin. She knew neither her mother nor her father and was raised by her grandmother, who she called Nanny because that's what she (the grandmother) was called by the white children for whose parents Nanny worked.

Janie indicates that she had no idea she wasn't white until she was around six years old, as she only played and associated with white children. And, she adds, she wouldn't have learned it then had it not been for a group picture taken by a photographer passing through the area.

Janie recalls that in the picture, there was a very dark little girl standing where she was supposed to be standing. Janie did not recognize the little girl as herself, and so she asked: "Where is me?"

This is a poignant moment in the novel and a poignant question overall, perhaps the question at the heart of all philosophical inquiry. In a world so complex and seemingly indifferent, the sense of who one is can get confused, misplaced, even lost altogether. Janie's question is a question we all ask from time to time. And if we do not have the support to help us understand where and who we are, we can find ourselves confused on this most fundamental of questions.

In his last book before his death, Buckminster Fuller wrote that Einstein believed two forces drive the evolutionary drama: fear and longing.[11] It is not hard to imagine that these two forces are at the heart of Janie's question. On the one hand, there is the fear operating in all of us from time to time that we are neither here nor there in any meaningful way—not seen, not recognized, not relevant or wanted. And on the other hand, there is the longing to be seen, heard, recognized, the longing to be a substantial and felt presence worthy of connection to something that matters.

In the above street scene, we also see both forces at play. The homeless person may feel fear of humiliation, rejection, and pain due to the need that drives the request. The passerby may be afraid of the embarrassment and awkwardness of the situation, and fearful of what could follow. The challenge for the passerby is the challenge implicit in several of the ethics (including the Wind Harp Ethic, the Personal Growth Ethic, and the Conscious Mistakes Ethic); she is left with determining whether or not she can behave respectfully, exhibiting respect for herself and for the other person, however she (the passerby) is treated. Her challenge—common to ethical dilemmas generally—is to see humanity in others while also exhibiting it in herself.

There are two points that may guide the passerby's response. First, there is the notion that we are not entirely our situation, any more than we are entirely the self or person that is visible to others. To be sure, the homeless individual is in a difficult situation. It is a situation that may dominate his life, but it is not the all of who he is. And to be treated as if we are only and entirely our situation can feel uncomfortable, disconcerting. In some cases, it can feel dishonoring. Nothing is more alienating than to be looked at but not seen, not recognized as a person behind whatever may lie on the surface. Even if our situation is not that of a homeless person but that of a wealthy landowner, an elected official, or a star athlete, it can feel tiresome to always be treated as if you are only your situation, only your role or station in life. Formalities exist, certainly. And based on the situation of the person in front of us (as we perceive it), we may for many good reasons respond in accord with standard protocols. These protocols help us get through our everyday dealings with others. But it is important to remember that there is a human being behind and within any situation, an observing self behind whatever mask is being worn. Holding this fact in mind makes us a little less likely to act robotically or stereotypically when addressing others, more likely to have flexibility and care in our dealings with them. This capacity—to look past the mask to the person wearing it—is at the heart of this dilemma and it foreshadows "the art of seeing" discussed in Part IV.

The second point that may guide the passerby's response is this: The ability to look past the mask to the person wearing it is a measure of how well we know ourselves.[12] And we know ourselves best by carefully observing and examining our own lives, our everyday strivings, the ways we have triumphed, and the ways we have avoided life's challenges. To look carefully at our lives is to see how we have changed over time and what was required of us in order to bring about that change. It is also to see our resistance to change even when reason called for it. We observe our past and perhaps current inclination to escape and avoid, as well as our occasional forthrightness. And we see how far we may live on occasion from our espoused ideals. To see into our lives in this way is to know ourselves more completely, with fewer misconceptions and far less denial. It is to acquire self-knowledge, and with such knowledge comes the understanding of how selves, any self, all selves, are made.

To say in reference to the homeless person (or anyone else for that matter), "I am nothing like him," is to offer too casual a response. The suggestion here is that as we come to know ourselves we see how similar we are to others. Potent factors separate us, yes, the situation into which we were born, our genetic propensities, the parenting and early schooling we received, all precede and influence our capacity for choice. We are not blank slates when we enter the world and we do not start out at the same place. We develop at different rates and the obstacles we face vary. Still, wherever we look, we see the luck of the draw and thus, versions of ourselves had things gone differently.

This realization does not prescribe exactly what should be done in this particular situation. As indicated above, there are simply too many variables. The exact response must be determined in the moment, in the sequence of moments that constitute the situation, as is true of all the dilemmas we have considered, each with its complexity stripped away so its core dynamics are visible and available for discussion. But it does increase the likelihood that the response, whatever it is, will have a greater degree of humanity in it, that it will have respect for self and other embedded in it, guiding the interaction through to its completion, though what is actually done may take many different forms. Conceptually, however, the issue is one of identity, knowing oneself to such an extent that we can see ourselves in others and others in ourselves. To the question, "Where is me?" the answer is, "Everywhere, or if not everywhere, then as far as my moral imagination will permit me to see."[13]

Scene Eight: "Lovers and Teachers"

An elderly woman, perhaps in her eighties, and her daughter meet at the mother's home.[14]

Daughter: Hi, Mom.

Mother: Hi, Honey.

Daughter: How are you, Mom? Are you doing OK?

Mother: Sure, great. Just great.

Daughter: It's a beautiful day.

Mother: Oh, it is, just a beautiful day. What did you do today, Honey?

Daughter: I had the most amazing day, Mom. I was given an award for my service to the community. It came as a complete surprise. The people at work arranged the whole thing. There was a formal presentation, people made speeches. I wish you could have been there. You would have been so proud of me.

Mother: That's wonderful, Honey, just wonderful.

Daughter: [Extended pause.] So, Mom, what are you fixing for yourself?

Mother: Well, I'm not sure . . .

Daughter: You're not sure?

Mother: Honey, how do you fix an egg?

Daughter: You don't remember how to fix an egg? [Pause.] Well, let's see. I think I can help you with that.

Mother: Oh, that would be great.

Daughter: No problem at all, Mom.

Mother: It's a beautiful day, isn't it?

Daughter: It sure is . . .

Mother: What did you do today, Honey?

Daughter: Mom! The award! The people at work . . .

Mother: Oh, yeah. The award. Who got the award?

Daughter: [Long pause.] Should we go for a walk, Mom?

Mother: That would be great.

Daughter: Margaret is coming this afternoon.

Mother: Margaret? Who is Margaret?

Daughter: She comes and spends the afternoon with you three days a week. You sing songs with her. You watch television, your favorite shows.

Mother: Do I like her?

Daughter: Yes, Mom, you're crazy about her. She's so nice.

Mother: I'd rather you stay. Can you stay? I don't want to be with a stranger.

Daughter: Margaret's not a stranger, Mom. She's part of our family now.

Mother: Oh.

Daughter: As soon as you see her, you'll remember. Margaret's a good person to spend time with.

Mother: [Pause.] It's a beautiful day, don't you think?

What are we to do with the heartbreaking losses that come our way: the loss of a job, divorce, the death of a loved one? In the above script, the mother is suffering from dementia, and by this fact alone, she presents her daughter with multiple challenges. The daughter is likely struck with a deep sadness. There are conversations certain now to go unfinished and loose ends never to be tied up. It is the beginning of a profound loss and although she may have friends and a family of her own, what to do about the situation seems, in her mind at least, to fall to her alone.

The degree to which we are prepared for such losses varies considerably. In this case, a relationship is changing. The daughter already feels the loss, and more is on the way. Frustration, despair, and even anger can result. Add to the situation the additional problem of limited financial resources, and the prospect of coping seems laughable. And yet here, as with all ethical dilemmas, is an opportunity (as wrong as that word may seem to the daughter at the moment). The Personal Growth Ethic states that it is ethical to continue to grow as a person; unethical to stop growing as a person. However understandable it might be for the daughter to throw up her hands and slide into despair over something about which, it seems, she can do very little—however understandable the frustration—this ethic announces that even here, in this most unfortunate of circumstances, is an opportunity for personal growth.

Human potential author Ken Keyes suggested that it is sometimes helpful to consider the world populated with only two kinds of people: lovers and teachers.[15] Lovers, he suggested, are those people who, through their interactions with us, introduce us to that "stuff" in ourselves (feelings, attitudes, abilities) that we love. Teachers, on the other hand, are those people who, through their interactions with us, introduce us to that stuff in ourselves that we do not love. Of course, some people do not affect us in either way. And with any long-term relationship, the individual with whom we are involved is no doubt both lover and teacher. This is simply a conceptual tool for turning our experience with others to our advantage. For while we may seek out lovers and avoid teachers, it is important to realize that our teachers are doing us an enormous service. They are helping us identify, albeit perhaps inadvertently, the behaviors, skills, attitudes, etc. that we need to acquire, accept, and/or change in order to be with the person in question without being uncomfortable or not quite ourselves.

It is not uncommon, for example, to hear people talk about how they dread the holidays with their family: "Because he makes me so upset!" "Because she drives me crazy!" It is a painful situation existing in many families, and one that can last for years until Keyes' conceptual tool (or something like it) is applied. What is the desirable skill, trait, or behavior I can learn from this teacher? What is it that if I could acquire it, or accept it, would allow me to be myself in that situation, without tension or anger? Perhaps it is the capacity to live and let live, to not take what is said personally, to say my truth forthrightly without defensiveness, to love unconditionally. To see the situation in those terms is to give us something to work on, with the ball in our court.

Even in situations in which problems between ourselves and others have seemingly become entrenched over the years, the realization that the other individuals involved are also teachers, whatever else they are (father, mother, sibling, coworker, etc.), can be helpful. It doesn't matter that they are unconscious of their role as teacher or that they are employing teaching methods we deplore. They nevertheless are helping us with our development, helping us to identify the skills, traits, behaviors, etc., that, if acquired, expand the range of situations and settings in which we can operate as ourselves, at ease, with less avoidance, fear, or blame.

In the above scene, the daughter, armed with Keyes' tool or some version of it, could ask, "What can I do—or perhaps learn to do—that would serve my Mother at this moment? The daughter may have all the motivation she needs to address fully and responsibly her Mother's situation. But if not, she can expand her perspective to include the realization that her felt duty is also an opportunity, that she is getting something in return however far from her mind and relatively unimportant that may seem to her at the moment. She is learning to be helpful and perhaps selfless to a degree she has never had to be before. She is being given the opportunity to witness herself being disciplined and flexible so as to ensure that uninterrupted care is provided; experiencing in herself, perhaps, a growing gratitude for life, for her Mother's life, and for her own life. She may see that for love's sake, or duty's sake, she is able to honor in nearly archetypic and timeless fashion a mother/daughter relationship. All of this in return for having overcome what for some could be paralyzing frustration and sadness in favor of a creative and loving use of the time remaining.

Scene Nine: "Realization and the Ongoing Dialogue"

Two brothers are engaged in conversation as they sit on a porch overlooking the countryside. It is a beautiful afternoon.

Murray: I figured it out!

Arnold: You figured what out?

Murray: The problem.

Arnold: You figured out "the problem"?

Murray: It came to me in a flash.

Arnold: The problem!

Murray: Well, maybe not *the* problem, maybe just my problem.

Arnold: [Kiddingly.] I didn't know you had a problem.

Murray: [Playing along.] You've always thought I had a problem.

Arnold: [Playfully.] Well, if you put it that way . . .

Murray: It's a relief in a way.

Arnold: And what, dare I ask, is your problem?

Murray: Well, I'm in shock.

Arnold: [Sarcastically.] Oh, brother!

Murray: It's the only thing I can think of to account for it.

Arnold: To account for what?

Murray: For the way I've been.

Arnold: And how have you been?

Murray: [Half laughing.] Let's not get into that!

Arnold: Shock, huh?

Murray: Shock.

Arnold: And what is responsible for this shock of yours?

Murray: You name it.

Arnold: Oh, come on!

Murray: No, really. You name it!

Arnold: [Sarcastically.] Being born!

Murray: Yes, maybe! Or when I was bullied. When I was made fun of . . . called ugly.

Arnold: You've got to be kidding!

Murray: Being rejected by Regina Jones in the fifth grade . . . Having to fight other kids. The death of our parents.

Arnold: This is just a part of life, Murray. Everyone . . .

Murray: When I saw how much some people have and how some people have nothing!

Arnold: [Losing patience.] You're a weakling!

Murray: These are shocking events, shocking things to experience.

Arnold: So life has you in shock!

Murray: And furthermore—

Arnold: Oh, no, I can see it coming . . .

Murray: —you're in shock, too.

Arnold: Oh, I suppose everyone is in shock?

Murray: Well, maybe not everyone.

Arnold: [Sarcastically.] The whole world is in shock!

Murray: No, not everyone. But these things are shocking . . . blows to the nervous system. Some part of us shuts down when they happen to us.

Arnold: Is this your effort to come up with an excuse for being a jerk? "Excuse me, Madam, I can't help it. I'm in shock!"

Murray: No, not at all.

Arnold: Then what's the point?

Murray: I'm just saying that a lot of shocking things happen to us. Even the things that you say are "just a part of life."

They're shocking . . . Like when you get shamed in front of other people, or when you realize—I mean really realize—that everyone you love is going to die.

Arnold: How about them Lakers!

Murray: You know what I'm saying.

Arnold: Maybe, but this is—

Murray: What am I saying?

Arnold: You're saying I need to stretch and take a walk!

Murray: No, for the sake of discussion, what am I saying?

Arnold: [Reluctantly.] Well, Doctor, you're saying we're shocked by some of the things that happen to us and we shut down.

Murray: Yes, exactly. We go unconscious, less vital and more absentminded.

Arnold: [Sarcastically.] We go unconscious—*really?*

Murray: And you're dealing with it, as well.

Arnold: [With exasperation.] I'm in shock? You can't let this be just about you? You have to drag me into it?

Murray: You're my brother, Arnold. I've known you my entire life. In my opinion—

Arnold: It's just life, Murray!

Murray: Yes, it's just life.

Arnold: [Sarcastically.] Big deal!

Murray: [Seriously.] I agree.

The challenges that confront these brothers are subtle. Murray has an insight. From the vantage point of this book, it doesn't matter if his insight is correct. It matters only that it may lead to a change in behavior or awareness that Murray finds useful. Life does give us insights. It yields gold if we seek it. And the Personal Growth Ethic states that we we must seek it, that it is our responsibility to continue to grow as persons, to deepen our understanding, and to reflect that understanding in our behavior. Murray has an insight, an additional way of understanding himself—greater self-knowledge, perhaps. And his challenge is to see if he can make this self-knowledge amount to something that matters, conduct that heals and/or reflects a more conscious, creative presence. His challenge is to turn his self-examination, his insight into greater ease with himself, greater capacity in the here and now, less absentmindedness.

Arnold's challenge is multilayered. Can he remain open, continue to consider his brother's line of thought, not escape from his discomfort (if that is what he feels) through any number of avoidance techniques he may have developed over the years—through humor, for example? The above exchange between the brothers may be their standard banter, a way of going back and forth that in no way discourages or avoids the topic. If so, then fine. The challenge for Arnold, however, is to remain open, especially given that Murray is suggesting that Arnold is also in shock. However absurd this notion seems to Arnold, it nevertheless is a notion that for Murray has merit. Philosopher Owen Barfield wrote: "With the eye you look at [the world]; with the imagination, you look into [it]."[16] Can Arnold suspend his skepticism, his resistance, long enough to consider Murray's ideas? Can he use his imagination, the great ally of both the Open-Mindedness Ethic and the Feedback Ethic, to discover personal truths if any reside there for him?

Arnold: Look, maybe you're on to something. I'm not saying you're not.

Murray: [With surprise.] You're giving in?

Arnold: [Setting his brother straight.] I'm your brother. I don't give in.

Murray: I'm just saying that we get crusty and stiff. We back ourselves into the same old routine. Our eyes glaze over.

Arnold: You're saying we're in shock.

Murray: We don't even know it. We get dulled by these shocking events, dulled and disorganized.

Arnold: [Kidding.] Maybe you're just describing yourself. You've been slipping, you know.

Murray: Yes, I'm describing myself.

Arnold: But that's not all you're saying.

Murray: No.

Arnold: You're saying it's also me.

Murray: *Shock* rings true to me, Arnold. I look around and everyone seems to have a degree of it.

Arnold: Everyone?

Murray: No, I suppose some people show no sign of it.

Arnold: But most people?

Murray: Maybe it's just me. But it's not a passing thought. I see it.

Arnold: Well, ah—

Murray: I don't think I knew what I was working on, or thinking about, until this idea hit me.

Arnold: You don't think you knew what you were thinking about? You *are* in trouble!

Murray: I think I was trying to get to this idea, or some idea that would allow me to understand why I am sometimes not present, *not fully there,* why I phase in and out. I was noticing that about myself, and it was bothering me.

Arnold: Come again?

Murray: You're right, though.

Arnold: I'm right?

Murray: It is a matter of what we do with the idea.

Arnold: [Holding the line.] I'm not doing anything. It's your idea!

Murray: This one has promise, Arnold.

Arnold: Maybe. Maybe for you.

Murray: I see things differently.

Once again, it doesn't matter if Murray's insight is in some sense correct or psychologically sophisticated. These are two brothers—friends, as well—sitting on a porch and discussing life, looking into life. One of them thinks he now knows more about himself than he knew before. He sees what previously he did not see, having observed something critical about himself. By degree, he is becoming more conscious. Even so, both he and his brother know that the insight matters little if it does not translate into new choices, a new capacity for follow-through. Both know that the insight must be actualized in order for it to be meaningful, especially if the measure is to remain human development and not simply the ability to weave ever more elaborate ways of accounting for past and future conduct.

Arnold: Shock. So you are in shock . . .

Murray: I've been coming out of it. That's what I think, enough, at least, to finally see it.

Arnold: And the upshot is . . .

Murray: I feel more aware of myself. I can do things I couldn't do before . . . at least I think I can.

Arnold: So how did this so-called insight dawn on you?

Murray: Well, to be honest, I was looking in the mirror and I—

Arnold: The mirror?

Murray: Yes, the mirror.

Arnold: [Sarcastically.] And . . .

Murray: I know this will sound crazy, but for a moment, just a quick moment, I saw that I wasn't all there.

Arnold: [Incredulous.] You're right. That is crazy. But if that's what you needed, I could have told you that!

Murray: Dismiss it if you like, Arnold, but—

Arnold: I'm just asking, Murray, that's all. I'm interested. Don't get me wrong. I'm your brother. I have a responsibility—

Murray: I feel looser, that's the thing. Freer. Like I've taken off my uniform. I'm enjoying the—

Arnold: OK, OK, but where do you go from here with this idea of yours, this new understanding, if that's what it is?

Murray: Well, I think I need to take this extra energy I'm feeling and put it into what I care about.

Arnold: Come again?

Murray: I think that's how it works. You have to use your insight, test it, live up to it in some way.

Arnold: Well, I—

Murray: You have to apply the understanding your insight gives you, especially if you want more.

Arnold: And so it goes?

Murray: Yes, exactly, and so it goes.

Arnold: I have no idea why I said that.

Murray: We're just talking here, Arnold. Like we always do. I'm glad for it. There's no one else to share this with, really.

Arnold: I'm with you, brother, no matter how crazy it gets.

Murray: It would seem nuts to me, too, if it hadn't hit me so hard. Dulled by the shocks of everyday life. That's what I'm saying has happened to me. To us.

As it turns out, Murray's insight is not about shock alone, but includes a way of proceeding, a way of traveling the Yellow Brick Road, though he doesn't put it that way. He offers his insight and then suggests that to honor the insight, he must act on it, test its value. If he does so, then perhaps more insight will follow. Murray argues implicitly for the Conscious Mistakes Ethic. If by whatever means we gain insight into ourselves—an increased understanding of who we are, of how we are made, of what we should do—then we must act in accord with our insight. In that way, life is lived somewhat more intentionally. Conduct is aligned with current awareness in order to test the value and limitations of that awareness.

Murray and Arnold are in a dialogue about personal growth or depth of understanding or self-realization. There are many ways to describe the topic. But however it is described, to have such a dialogue—over years, with one or more individuals—is, from the human logic point of view, a form of wealth. Such dialogues are as important as the insights they permit us to discuss. Through the Conscious Mistakes Ethic and through the ethics of human development in general, we take ourselves to the very frontier of our development. From there we travel on our own, aided by insight and by the dialogues we engage in with our fellow travelers. These dialogues may be full of playfulness, full of laughter, teasing, even testing, but at base, they force clarity where fuzziness exists and perspective when it is clear we have taken ourselves too seriously. They enrich our experience of the journey—indeed, they help us remain committed to the journey—and on occasion permit us to experience the joy of advanced development while at the same time remaining on average a long way from it.

The challenges/dilemmas embedded in the exchange between Murray and Arnold are varied. On the one hand, there is the Conscious Mistakes Ethic, with the added requirement that consciousness must continue to expand. *Align conduct with an ever-expanding consciousness, and therein lies method for the realization of inherent possibilities*. But there is another ethic alluded to as well, though obliquely: the Sustainability Ethic. After the moment of insight and as we labor through conduct to explore its worth, we must find ways to sustain our effort. Dialogue is one of those ways: dialogue with trusted friends, with individuals who understand in their own way and on their own terms the nature of the topic. And if they happen to understand the topic better than we do, all the better. Through dialogue comes co-mentoring, refinement of thought, emotional support: essential nourishment for sustaining the realization of potential. The task is to cultivate and nurture the art of such dialogues, sustaining them so that they can sustain us. In principle, such a task should not be difficult. According to one of the assumptions underlying this book, everyone wants the same thing. After the worry and distraction are cleared away, after a certain comfort level is obtained or in moments of reflection, it is the realization of inherent possibility that is on everyone's mind, in one way or another.

SUMMARY

There are many other dilemmas that we could consider here. Everyday life is full of them, some small (or seemingly so), others with implications reaching well beyond the immediate sphere of family and work. The overriding point, however, is that ethical dilemmas are defining. They are potential turning points for the individuals involved and for the society and culture of which the individuals are a part. The capacity to behave ethically is exercised or not in such moments, and the environment that supports ethical conduct is altered, however slightly. Challenges and dilemmas like the ones depicted here involve us in the change process. Whatever our station in life, they give us the opportunity, if we so choose, to participate in the development of both our selves and our society. To say that life is a morality play is to say, simply, that life is inevitably populated by dilemmas of one sort or another, and that these dilemmas have developmental implications for the characters involved and for the ongoing play.

The dilemmas considered here attempt to cover central themes (choice, for example, or continuous personal development), but the examples used to illustrate these themes could have varied considerably. In one scene, anger and resentment are passed from one person to the next in a work setting, but the issue or problem is common to society at large. In another scene, a daughter deals with the loss of her mother, but loss visits everyone and takes many forms. The point is that these are examples. While we may not have experienced any of them in our own lives exactly as presented here, everyday life is certain to send us variations on these themes.

We turn now to issues only alluded to in the above examples.

Part IV

The Ideas with Which We See

"Our circumstances are not merely the facts of life as we meet them, but also, and even more, the ideas in our minds. It is impossible to obtain any control over circumstances without first obtaining control over the ideas in one's mind."[1]

—E. F. Schumacher
A Guide for the Perplexed

The Open-Mindedness Ethic states that each person's view is necessarily incomplete,[2] and that it is ethical to remain open to the possibility that more information could result in a more complete and accurate view. This applies to our view of others as well as to our view of life. We see only a part, not the whole. Other legitimate views could and no doubt do exist. This is a point worth remembering because the view we hold of others necessarily influences our involvement with them.[3]

THE ART OF SEEING

If, for example, we see the person or persons with whom we are involved as an enemy, then we are more likely to behave in certain ways than if we were to see them as a friend or ally. Our personal history, along with the specifics of the situation, will and should inform our view. But the suggestion here (and presumed in the previous discussion of lovers and teachers) is that our view of others can be chosen, selected perhaps from a set of alternative views. This is key because, as suggested above, how we choose to view others is among the important choices we make in our everyday involvement with them.

This is not to suggest that we adopt a view of others that is simplistic or naive, or that we ignore the insights and subtle discriminations life has offered us. Rather, the suggestion here is that we choose the view that we adopt, and that we do so consciously, deliberately, since it affects the likelihood of what follows. Too often, we do not make this choice consciously. Instead, it falls by default to established habits of viewing, habits of seeing the world and others in a particular way—what we might think is the only way in which we can or should see them.

This brings us back to the observing self, in this case to seeing the ideas with which we see,[4] the organizing categories with which and into which we sort our experience and, in particular, our experience of others. Often the ideas with which we see remain unconscious for the longest time, operating in us as if they are inseparable from us. But they are separable. Though we see through and with them, they nevertheless are acquired. Like glasses we have forgotten we have on, the ideas with which we see are a part of the self that is created. Everyday experience has shaped and molded them. And they typically remain in place unless some experience comes along to challenge their adequacy, some experience that we cannot understand or account for with our existing categories. Until then, the glasses appear to be working just fine, and so we increasingly lose any awareness we have of them as separate from ourselves. The prospect of seeing others differently hardly seems a matter of choice.

But when we step back, as contact with the observing self requires, it is possible to see even ingrained, hard-to-see ideas and categories, possible to witness our habits of thinking and viewing. By this step alone, choice enters the equation. The ideas and categories become objects or tools that we, as subject, can manipulate and utilize for desired ends. Rather than allowing the conditioning of the past to determine our view of others, choice anchored to principle (which is also chosen) can gain a foothold.

It may be, for example, that the person with whom we are dealing is different from us in any number of ways, some of which are easy to accept, and others not at all. It may be that we have had a difficult history with the person in question—strained, unpleasant, even contentious. Still, the suggestion is that it is possible to transcend history[5] and those particular associations and see the person in ways that allow the best of what is in us to come out—not blindly and not so as to make us victims of good intentions, but consciously, with a command of self on display.

Yes, the person in front of us may be a bully, a power monger, a snob. He may be selfish, dismissive, ruthless, or off-the-wall. But whatever the specific behavior, it is fair to say that the person in question, like us, is attempting to deal as effectively as he knows how (although perhaps with little success) with the challenges of a life out of balance, an existence that is almost unbelievable, that delivers in unequal measure, and that could end at any moment. Even so, the person in question wants what we all want: to be treated with respect; to be recognized, understood, and accepted; to be seen in a generous and forgiving light. That is what the person in front of us wants and what he is attempting to secure, though the means employed may be terribly inept or even distorted.[6]

This view of others is as valid as any other in most situations. And to adopt this view, or some variation of it, is to allow another understanding to enter the formula, a compassion that can perhaps take some of the destructiveness out of our engagement with others. There may be situations where this view is not appropriate. But making our view a conscious choice is what is being emphasized here (as with the lovers and teachers metaphor).

The point is this: When we begin to understand the ideas with which we see—our own organizing categories—we thereby make them available for consideration. At that point, as we consider and evaluate their worth, we may find that we are confronted with a deeply important decision, one with profound implications for the resolution of conflict, the strengthening of character, the quality of our everyday discourse. After thinking about it, will we choose to leave our view as it is? Or will we choose to modify it as best we can because by so doing we believe we increase the likelihood of an ethical, creative, peaceful exchange? Will we adopt a view, as accurate as any other, that relaxes our defensiveness, our guardedness, and allows other parts of us, other behaviors, to surface? Or will we hold on to our existing view, perhaps accurate in one way, perhaps limiting, hold on to it because the person or persons involve deserve no better, or because we deserve no better. It is a choice, and with such choices we certainly don't determine but we do influence the outcome of our exchanges with others.

THE RIGHT IDEAS IN MIND

This raises another issue fundamental to the resolution of the dilemmas that come our way, a companion issue or extension of the one just discussed. Even if ethical dilemmas are recognized for what they are (i.e., as self-making opportunities—discussed in Part V), even if the consequences for retreating from them or failing to meet them constructively are understood, even if we practice with some regularity the fine art of seeing (as discussed above), it is still possible to be pulled off course by our bad habits, our appetite for the immediate at the expense of the longer term. Why? There are many reasons, but here the focus is on just one: the quality or nature of the ideas we have in mind.

When it comes to making decisions or choices, one of the variables about which we might do quite a lot is what we have in mind at the moment we make those decisions. If, for example, we have a particular hurt in mind perhaps from a betrayal or affront, then we lean our decision-making and, thus, our behavior in the direction of self-and other-destructiveness. If instead we have our most deeply held values in mind, those things that in moments of reflection we say we stand for, then we lean our decision-making in the direction of the self-and other-honoring. What we have in mind at the moment we make our decisions matters. We may not be conscious of what we have in mind. We may be so distracted or full of conflict that we cannot begin to articulate it. But we do have something in mind, even if it is poorly formed, unclear, or confused.

In common parlance, the question frequently asked after someone has done something particularly foolish or destructive is, "What was he thinking?" It is a question that recognizes in popular terms the same point being made here. When choice points arrive (and they arrive continuously), what we have in mind influences to some degree the choices we make.

It might be useful and appropriate to pause here and acknowledge that the moment-to-moment exchange between person and environment is made of three parts. There is the moment as we find it, *consisting in part of the ideas we have in mind*. There is the behavior we choose to engage in. And there are the consequences that follow. The ideas held in mind exert their influence and then are influenced by the consequences that result from what we choose to do. It is this ongoing interaction with the environment that over time makes us who we are. And the ideas we have in mind, our mindset, to use another term, is one element in this interaction. And yet, it is the element on which a life with purpose and intention greatly depends. What we think and value at any given moment affects what we will choose to do in that moment. Effective "piloting" requires, among other things, that we keep our values in mind, "our head on straight," a challenging task depending on the situation we are facing and depending as well on our "habits of mind." But habits can be broken and new, healthier habits put in their place. And in some respects that is what we are talking about here: cultivating the habit of keeping the right ideas and values in mind so that we increase the probability that we will steer our lives in accord with those ideas and values. Mindset is only one part of the equation but to neglect it is to make less likely choices consistent with our purpose. Ultimately, to neglect the contents of the mind as decision points arrive is to invite drift and thus, the likelihood of a longer, less certain route to desired ends.

That said, how can we keep the ideas in mind that increase the likelihood that we will choose to behave in accord with our long-term interests, not falling prey to short-term distractions at the expense of our values and continued development? Many programs (and cultural institutions, for that matter) face this issue straight on. Twelve-step programs, for example, help participants keep their commitment to sobriety in mind. By attending a meeting each week (or even several meetings each week, if necessary), the twelve-step participant acquires a language, a view, a set of ideas, and so, overall, a new history that begins to compete with the old one; a set of "ideas-in-mind" that make the decision to drink less likely when the next opportunity arrives. (Of course, the individual may drink. He may fall off the wagon. But he now has not only a support system encouraging his sobriety, he also has reasons for not drinking more often in mind. Other factors may prevail but he now meets the temptation to drink with a different mindset, one that may influence a break with his previous pattern.)

Life coaching systems also employ methodologies for keeping one's values, or perhaps one's vision or goal in mind; techniques for calling to mind the values the individual would most like to have expressed in her behavior.[7] These techniques do not guarantee that the practitioner's behavior will express the intended value(s). But they are an explicit recognition of the notion that what we have in mind the moment we make decisions is consequential, influencing not only the decisions we make but also the options we consider available. Again, the methodology or technique may not work. Other factors may control the moment. But we increase the probability of behavior in accord with our espoused values because those values are now in mind.

In truth, sports coaches, military and religious leaders, psychologists, parents, etc., also use this methodology. It is, in a sense, the socializing methodology of society's institutions. All attempt to put the right ideas (in their view) in mind—ideas that serve the cause of their institution, team, or society, but ideas that may also serve the individual in her life beyond the institution.

In his book *A Guide for the Perplexed*, economist E. F. Schumacher points out that yoga "according to the greatest of yoga teachers, Patanjali [c. 300 BC] . . . is [about] the control of the ideas in the mind."[8] Schumacher argues that yoga, meditation, and continuous inner prayer are all techniques for obtaining control over the ideas held in mind, whatever else their purpose.[9] To these techniques should be added the many techniques developed by modern psychology to accomplish the same end.[10] All are designed to quiet the chattering mind, allowing us to focus on and more readily see its activity. They are techniques in service to the observing self, techniques that permit and implicitly encourage observation, the witnessing of mental life and, through that witnessing, the realization that we are not one and the same with it. And thus, that our mental life can be managed, placed in service to ends we truly desire. Modern psychology, like any number of other disciplines, is interested in the release of potential that comes when identity expands beyond the contents of the mind and those contents are managed for ethical ends.[11]

When anger and hate are the focus of one's mental life, when getting even, the worthlessness of others, or the worthlessness of oneself are the ideas continuously held in mind, then troublemaking is likely to occur. Dilemmas, choice points in general, whether large or small, have less chance of being resolved ethically because the ideas in mind are not the right ideas for bringing about a better world.

This is not to say that there isn't plenty to be angry about, or that one is not right to be troubled or even enraged by what goes on in this world. These are understandable reactions, and healthy in a sense. But we often make things worse when we act out due to these emotions and ideas. This is the Wind Harp Ethic, the transforming of anger and resentment into conduct that instead of leading to more injustice and destruction, leads to consciously selected ethical ends. And one of the ways this transformation occurs is through the management of the mind, the management of the ideas one keeps in mind, surrounding or replacing the negative with the ideas or values that make ethical conduct more likely. To the art of seeing, we now add the art of setting the occasion, the art of putting in mind as continuously as needed the ideas, concepts, and values we would have guide us as we operate in the world.[12]

PAIN, SUFFERING, AND VALUED BEHAVIOR

One problem fundamental to a discussion of ethics is the way in which our lives can be governed not by the pursuit of personal development but by escape and avoidance. We do not wish to suffer pain, anxiety, or undo discomfort, and so we avoid situations similar to those that have been associated with those experiences in the past. This makes perfect sense in all cases except those where the situations in question stand between us and our development as persons. Those situations must be addressed even though some degree of pain, suffering, and sacrifice may be involved. Otherwise, there is no personal growth, no realization of dreams, goals, or inherent possibilities.

Certainly, some degree of pain and suffering is an inevitable part of life.[13] They come our way by virtue of the fact that we are beings conscious of our own very limited and fragile existence, beings with sensitive nervous systems that allow us to feel deeply, to register the slightest loss, and to anticipate and even dread the harshness of what we believe to be around the bend. We are certain to lose loved ones; certain to see those we care about suffer; certain to lose our youth, our innocence, our physical capacity. Certain, that is, if we are fortunate enough to live a full lifetime. There is illness and infirmity, and there is injustice, the enormous disparities in this world that we cannot view directly without some degree of nausea. Pain, loss, and suffering in some measure are an inevitable part of life, but we need not add to them unnecessarily. That is the point emphasized here. And we should not yield invariably to their influence as decision points arrive.

Psychologist Steven Hayes defines valued behavior[14] as behavior consistent with our dreams and aspirations, in accord with our values and principles. From the point of view of this book, it is behavior that furthers our development as persons. Hayes offers the following: As we proceed with valued behavior, we discover that it necessarily induces a larger context within which to place our experience, including our suffering—a context that, because of what we have achieved through valued pursuits, also includes joy, the sense of accomplishment, feelings of fulfillment. We do not eliminate pain and suffering as we continue to engage in valued behavior. Nor are they denied or ignored. Rather, we place them in a wider context that allows us to see them as a part of, but not the whole of, our existence.

The problem with pain and suffering is that they are experienced in such an intimate way—in our stomach lining, in fraying nerves, for the longest time in the private conversations we have with ourselves about ourselves. The resulting experience is so personal that we can consider them the truth of our existence. Only by persisting with valued behavior—this continues Hayes's point—do we separate ourselves from suffering to the extent that it can be witnessed, accepted, and honored in whatever way is appropriate, but no longer felt to be the whole of who we are or the whole of life. Indeed, by so persisting, we give ourselves evidence of the fact that it is not the whole of life. Through conduct focused on the realization of inherent possibilities, on our dreams, goals, and aspirations, we announce to ourselves that our suffering is not the entirety of who we are. We give ourselves a foothold from which the pain and suffering can be seen by an ever-more-stable and present observing self and, thus, by a self that does not identify with the suffering to such an extent that the suffering drives decision-making. Rather, we evolve a new sturdiness, a greater capacity to remain on purpose. The suffering is contained and accepted as one continues to behave in accord with espoused values.[15]

This is a return to the Pain-Directed Ethic, and perhaps to an enlarged understanding of it. We deal with the pain and suffering in our lives not by ignoring them or avoiding them, but by addressing them. And one of the ways we address them is by continuing to behave in accord with what we believe to be required for our continued development and fulfillment as persons. We deal with them by continuing to engage in valued behavior.

It is, of course, very difficult to always behave in accord with one's values, especially when our fears encourage us to withdraw or retreat. And it is only with some hesitancy that any course of action can be recommended at all as some people have had to endure enormous pain and suffering. And yet, this is the course argued for here simply because it marks the route that makes it less likely that we will add to our suffering unnecessarily. And further, because it is the route that will allow us to find whatever joy and fulfillment is ours to obtain. It is ethical to proceed with valued behavior and to do so despite the fact that stress, suffering, and sacrifice may be involved. Considerable trust and resolve are likely to be required by this stratagem. And for some people, because of the pain and suffering they have had to endure, there is, perhaps, something approaching the heroic, as well.

Hayes makes his point by means of the following analogy: "You've been driving a bus called 'your life,' and along the way, you've picked up passengers . . . some you like, some you do not like. These are your memories, bodily sensations, conditioned emotions, programmed thoughts, historically produced urges, and so on." You've picked up a lifetime of experiences and these experiences "speak to you," they have voices, they are "on the bus." And at every fork in the road, each has an opinion. Some may be screaming to stop or go forward, to take this turn and not that one; but as Hayes points out, they are passengers. You are driving the bus, and you have a very important decision to make: to choose to drive in the direction of your values, the things you say you stand for, to drive in the direction of your own development as a person, or to drive in the direction that will allow some of your passengers to avoid their fears. The former, writes Hayes, is "the path of vulnerability and risk, but it is about something . . . There is a distinction," he continues, "between you, the conscious driver of the bus, and the passengers you carry. You have room on the bus for them. You accept them. You defuse from them.[16] But then you turn your eyes back to the road and connect with that which you really value. You drive in that direction. As a result, your life grows a little, and it becomes a little more vital and flexible."[17]

We all have histories. And by the time we wake up and become aware of how our individual history has affected us, we can find that we have acquired an approach to life that is as much about escape and avoidance as it is about our values, aspirations, and goals. Or we can wake up to the fact that we have simply been wrongheaded, living in pursuit of what we do not truly value. Either way, we discover that we may need to reorient our lives, become more self-directing, acquire the skills and the strength to persist in the direction of our deepest values even though our history may call us in another direction.

If we do persist, however, even though stress and sacrifice (behavioral fences, for example, as defined in Ethic 9) may be involved, then the beneficiaries of our efforts are not ourselves alone. The difference we make for ourselves is a difference we make for others, in some cases for others we never see or touch directly. This is because we live within a social fabric, and to genuinely affect the fabric is to affect all those within it. This is the last point for consideration in Part IV: how the resolving of the dilemmas that come our way or the pursuit of valued behavior in general reaches beyond those with whom we are involved directly to the larger community—not magically, but because we are connected to one another in ways that are nearly obvious when we stop to think about it.

THE CENTER OF GRAVITY

Philosopher Ken Wilber defines the concept of a center of gravity as follows:

> Every society has a certain center of gravity . . . around which the culture's ethics, norms, rules, and basic institutions are organized, and this center of gravity provides the basic cultural cohesion and social integration for that society.
>
> This cultural center of gravity acts like a magnet on individual development. If you are below the average level, it tends to pull you up. If you try to go above it, it tends to pull you down. The cultural center of gravity acts as a pacer of development—a magnet—pulling you up to the average expectable level of consciousness development. Beyond that, you're on your own, and lots of luck, because now the magnet will try to drag you down.[18]

With this concept, we are connected. The behavior of the individual is linked to the health and vitality of the culture overall (as illustrated below). That is its elegance, and one of the reasons it is so useful.

For example, every organization—every family, workplace, and local community—has a culture, and thus its own center of gravity. If we enter a workplace with a performance standard below the standard already established, then the forces operating within that workplace—peer pressure, new employee orientation, staff training, etc.—will operate on us so as to raise our performance to the established standard sooner than otherwise would occur. The center of gravity, acting like a magnet, pulls us up.

On the other hand, if we enter that workplace with a performance standard above the established standard, then the forces at play—peer pressure, lack of support for high performance, resistances of one sort or another—will tend to pull us down. Though by our behavior we point the workplace in the direction it should evolve, we do so at some cost to

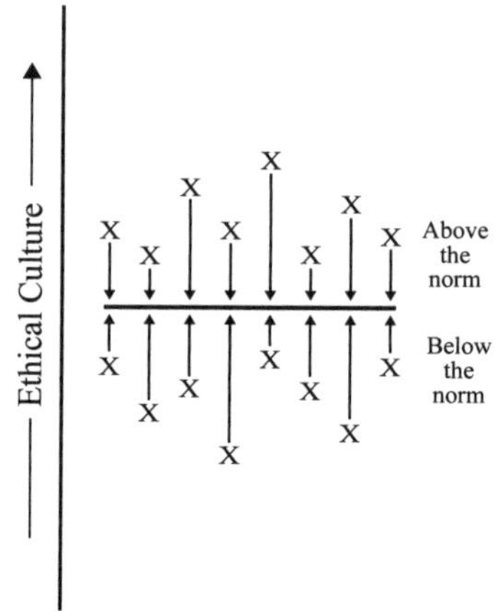

Figure 1: A graphic depiction of an organization's center of gravity. The *Xs* represent the average performance levels of the individuals comprising the organization.

our own energy since the center of gravity, acting like a magnet, drags us down. Figure 1 depicts the effect of the center of gravity on individual performance in a workplace or organization.

However, the reverse is also true: Just as the center of gravity exerts its effect on individual performance, so individual performance exerts its influence on the center of gravity. Other things being equal, when individual performance improves, the center of gravity rises. When individual performance declines, the center of gravity falls.

Figure 2 displays an organizational center of gravity that has risen over time as one or more individuals in the organization raise their performance level(s).[19]

Now, perhaps the organization depicted in Figure 2 is merely one of many such organizations in the community, all addressing the same issue. Suppose further that these organizations are in contact with one another, that in various ways they work together (examples could include social service agencies working on homelessness or child abuse; departments within a large governmental agency; or businesses within the same industry, competitors on one level but collaborators when it comes to issues that affect the industry as a whole). Within this network of organizations, it is reasonable to assume that there exists a cultural center

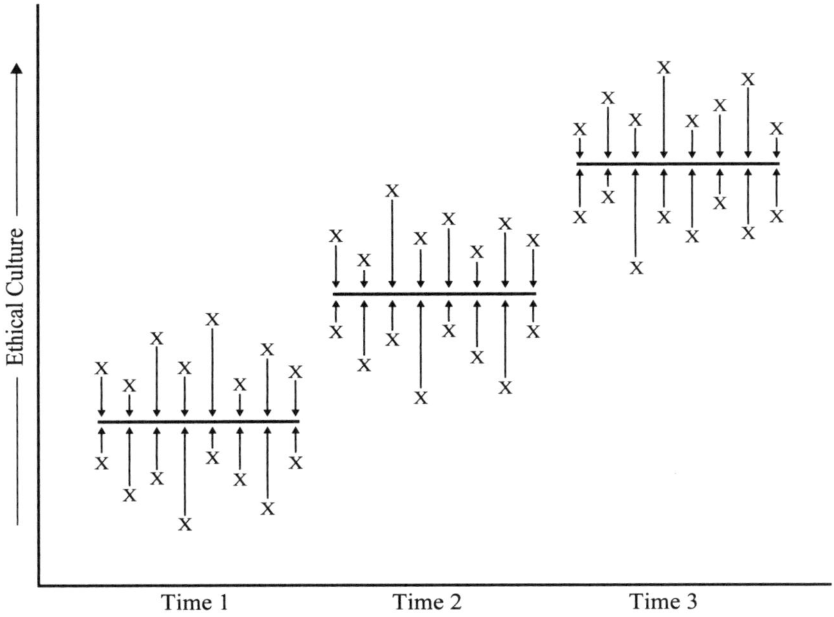

Figure 2: An organizational center of gravity rising over time as one or more organizational members (*X*s) raise their performance standard(s).

of gravity and that this center of gravity operates on and is responsive to organizational performance in the same way that the center of gravity within a single organization operates on and is responsive to individual performance.

If an organization enters this network operating below the network's established standard, then the forces operating within the network (i.e., collegial associations, established standards for products and services, accreditation processes, etc.) serve to raise the performance of that organization in the direction of the network standard sooner than otherwise would occur.

On the other hand, if the organization enters the network operating above the network's standard, then it must maintain its higher standard largely on its own. Though by its performance it points the network in the direction it should evolve, it does so at some cost to its resources, as it is now using its energy in part to counter the pull of a lower standard.

At the same time, the performance of the organizations within the network affects the network's standard, just as a single organization's standard is affected by the performance of individuals within it. Figure

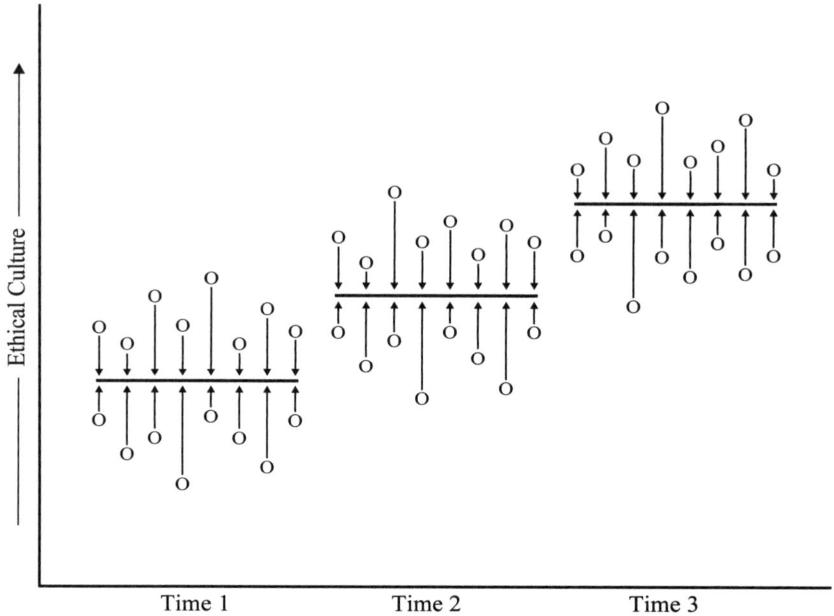

Figure 3: The center of gravity in a network of organizations rising over time as one or more organizations (*O*s) within the network raise their center(s) of gravity.

3 depicts the rise in the center of gravity of a network of collaborating organizations as one or more organizations within the network raise their standard(s).

Finally, a community has a cultural center of gravity operating on network performance in the same way that a network's center of gravity operates on organizational performance (and an organization's center of gravity operates on individual performance). If a given network performs below the community's established standard, then the network's performance is pulled up sooner than would occur otherwise. If the network performs above the community's standard, then it must rely more fully on motivations and supports interior to itself since the effect of the communitywide center of gravity is to drag down the network's performance. The high-performing network may be appreciated—its performance, a source of community pride—but the community's established standard does not support the network's higher standard and, over time, will tend to drag it down.

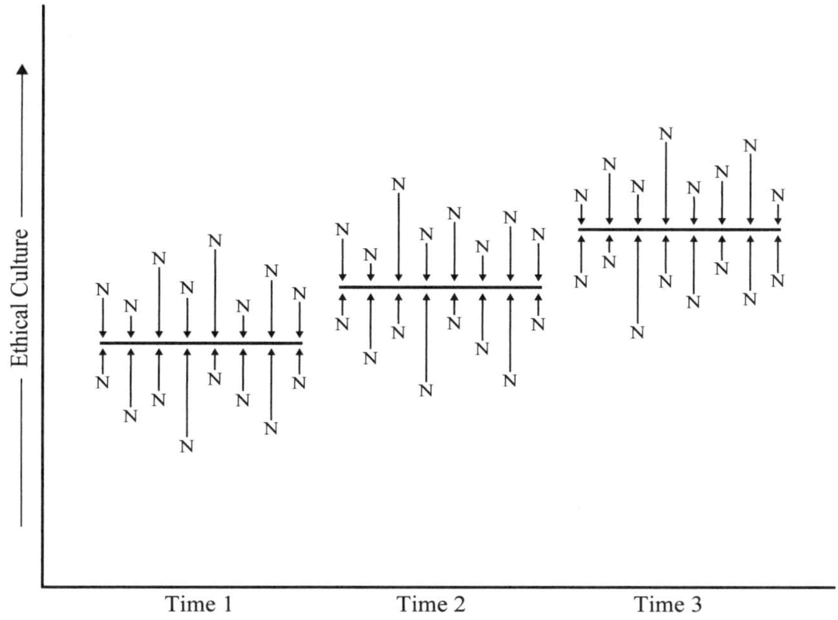

Figure 4: The center of gravity in a community rising over time as one or more networks (*N*s) within the community raise their center(s) of gravity.

On the other hand, if a single network raises its performance, then (other things being equal) the overall center of gravity in the community will rise. If, for example, a network of organizations contending with the issue of homelessness or health care or education raises its overall standard, serving its mission more effectively, more creatively, more ethically, then the center of gravity in the entire community will rise—perhaps only by degree, but rise nonetheless. Figure 4 depicts the rising center of gravity in a community as one or more networks within that community raise their standard(s).

Thus, by means of their centers of gravity, organizations, networks, and communities each exert their influence on their constituent parts; each part, in turn, exerting its influence on the evolving standard. Through our willingness to address the dilemmas that come our way, continuing with valued behavior despite the difficulty, we affect others, sometimes directly but also, by the above logic, through a standard that we help establish.

To expand slightly the above line of thought, it is appropriate to note that it is certainly very difficult to know the exact reach of any one ethically resolved dilemma. Maybe the location of the cultural center of gravity (in the family, workplace, or community) is not affected in any significant way, the social impact washed away by any number of factors with no one affected except, perhaps, the person addressing the dilemma. However, when we witness or otherwise learn of an ethically resolved dilemma, even if the standard in the organization of which we are a part is not affected, we are frequently moved. The part well played earns our admiration and may cause us to reflect on our own standard(s). We are at times emboldened by what we see is possible for others. The exact or full reach of the ethically resolved dilemma is difficult to know, but it is not unreasonable to presume that in the resolving of the dilemma, we are benefitting others within the larger social fabric and not just ourselves.

SUMMARY

This book is about the difficult journey from childhood to whatever level of maturity and enlightenment is ours to obtain. It is about the journey of the self, a journey marked by the tests of heart and mind that serve as a measure of development. These tests are self-making in nature. They are the means by which we strengthen and evolve ourselves while also strengthening the organizations and communities of which we are a part.

The ideas we hold in mind, the ideas with which we see and meet the world, can aid us in the resolution of these tests. *Mindfulness* might be the term, the capacity to hold in mind the values we would have our behavior express. Perhaps a better term is simply *self-control*, the government of the self, the ability to engage in valued behavior even though our history and immediate environment may not support that behavior, and indeed may be at odds with it.

The ethics of human development provide guidance. They prescribe the conduct certain to educate, mature, and enlighten us, certain therefore to lead to the tests of heart and mind on which development depends. As suggested in Part I, the ethics of human development—along with the resolution of the dilemmas and challenges that come our way—are the means by which we travel the Yellow Brick Road.

Down that road, and with every step, lies the increase in ethical creativity we can offer those we care about and the organizations of which we (and they) are a part. The maturity we are after is absent victimhood, bad faith, and the blaming of others, and is characterized increasingly by a willingness and desire to play the non–zero sum game, a game wherein actions benefit not only ourselves but also an ever-larger circle of others. The capacity to play this game is an inherent possibility, connecting self-interest to the development of others. And, importantly, the actual playing of the game is the life artist theme come back around, i.e., detachment within involvement; the pursuit of valued behavior; a self made large enough to contain its entire history—its joy and its suffering—without that history deterring it from its purpose.

Part V

The Theater of Change

"It is an early spring evening in a semi-darkened warehouse in New York near the docks. The hour has passed at which Robert Whitman's theatre work 'Light Touch' was to have begun. People are still buying tickets . . .

Awaiting the performance, we sat in the damp and gloom, uneasy over the continued delay . . .

Then a strange event of disclosure occurred—a disclosure of disclosure. In the darkness, the main door of the warehouse in the middle of the wall before us slowly rolled up and opened. It went from floor to ceiling . . . the sounds of the city could be heard . . . and cars appeared occasionally, framed by the door, as they passed on the street directly outside. Appeared, but appeared transfigured, as if a spell had been cast over them. Details of their shape and movement, ordinarily not noticed leapt out . . . It was as if cars were being seen for the first time . . . The driver's intent gaze on the road in front of him chipped out merely a fragment of the world in which he moved.

After a car had passed by in this side street, the space in which we were living would relax and expand again to admit the sounds of the vast city—Then again, as if we inhabited a breathing organism, events on the street would take prominence. Slowly and majestically, matters unleafed through time, yet also sadly, as if all of us—rapt and silent inside the warehouse—were aware that the spell that had been cast was fragile. One felt grateful to be alive and conscious."[1]

—Bruce Wilshire
Role Playing and Identity

The focus of Part V is on the training program developed to teach the ethics of human development, the methods used, and the rationale behind the program. Here are the basic assumptions shared with participants at the start of training:

> Assumption #1: The individual or organization inviting this training is a healthy individual/organization; healthy enough to know that improvements are always possible, even when—especially when—it comes to ethical conduct.
>
> Assumption #2: No one lives a totally ethical life; we all have improvements we could make. This training program is about the advantages that might accrue were we to make even slight improvements.
>
> Assumption #3: To get the most out of this training, the emphasis throughout must be not on how others in our lives or in the organization are doing with respect to these ethics, but on "how I am doing"; the emphasis and focus must be on oneself.
>
> Assumption #4: The purpose of training is served best when participants feel safe, comfortable, their own current views honored; for this reason, participants are encouraged not to accept the ethics of human development uncritically, but to examine, discuss, and reflect on them, to treat them at the very least as a whetstone against which to sharpen and refine their own ethics if the ethics of human development prove inadequate to their needs.

These assumptions are important because the topic of ethics is a personal one. Room must be made within the training experience for each person to find her own way to the relevance of the material. Only then is it possible to embrace the next higher standard, whether that standard is the one provided by the ethics of human development or a standard of one's own making.

The training experience is highly interactive and incorporates the following components:

Presentation and discussion. Each ethic is presented to and discussed by participants.

Image theater. Participants engage in exercises designed to bring the ethics and related concepts to life.

Role-playing. Participants are given the opportunity to improvise solutions to ethically challenging situations (examples of which were provided in Part III).

Workbook. Through workbook questions and exercises, participants clarify the personal/behavioral meaning of each ethic and, in the process, determine their own ethical conduct objectives.

The image theater component of the training program draws extensively from the work of Brazilian theatrical scholar August Boal[2] and American family therapist Virginia Satir.[3] Both have pioneered the image theater concept, documenting its power to reveal and inspire. Several exercises within the program are drawn from their work and modified to address specific training issues, while other exercises are unique to this program. Together, these exercises give participants a graphic, visual understanding of the nature of organizations; the fundamental tension between individual expression and teamwork (i.e., between rights and responsibilities); the limited nature of any one person's view; choice and "bad faith"; continuous personal growth; and other issues necessarily related to human development.

The role-playing component[4] is comprised of scripted scenes read by two or more volunteer participants. Each scene reveals the absence of one or more of the ethics of human development. Script topics, several of which were discussed in Part III, include breaking the rules, resistance to change, pretending one is being forced to work, engaging in blame and recrimination, passing anger and resentment on to others, the improper or insensitive delivery of feedback, etc. If the training is being provided to a specific organization, then scripts are selected in advance and new scripts are written to speak to the immediate needs of the organization.

In addition, scripts are tailored through modifications in language and situation to reflect the everyday life of the organization in question.

When enacted, the role-playing scenes set the occasion for a useful and often clarifying discussion. However, the task is not simply to have a clarifying discussion—to have, for example, the missing ethic or ethics identified and possible solutions discussed—but rather to have proposed solutions enacted in the scene. Therefore, at various points in the discussion, participants are invited to take the place of one of the actors and to complete the scene in a way more in keeping with the ethics of human development. The job of the actor or actors remaining in the scene is to stay in character, not blindly but rather resisting the enactment of the proposed solution in a way that invites the person enacting the solution to use all of his strength. The result for that person is practice in the difficult art of creating and improvising ethical solutions on the spot.

The image theater and role-playing exercises are built on the assumption that the most unforgettable and personally beneficial of all forms of theater is the theater in which we choose to act, the theater that addresses our problems and in which we (along with friends, colleagues, and coworkers) work to find a solution. These exercises—the scripted scenes, the exercises revealing the meaning of complex concepts—invite participants to overcome their hesitancy and act on behalf of their own view and, by so doing, to give themselves a hard-to-forget experience, one that they will review and perhaps mull over, hopefully altering and enhancing their readiness to behave more effectively when similar situations arise in the future.

The workbook used in conjunction with the training allows participants to personalize the meaning of each ethic and to identify what must be done in either one's personal life or in the organization, if one is to behave in accord with the ethics of human development. It is by means of the workbook that participants emerge from training with individualized ethical conduct objectives—actions or steps that they feel are consistent with their understanding of the requirements of the ethics of human development. These can be simple action items, such as "Give Harry the feedback on his performance that I have been avoiding giving him" or "Have the discussion with my team about the division of responsibilities," etc.

On some occasions, a "One Week Report" is compiled and returned to the organization after the program. This report lists the ethical conduct objectives undertaken and completed as of the one-week mark following training. Created via self-report, with anonymity protected, this report documents the immediate or short-term benefits of training. Its name derives from the fact that unless participants act within one week on an issue that they identified as important during training, the probability of them ever doing so is much reduced.

At the end of training, participants complete a questionnaire in which they rate their satisfaction with themselves and with the organization overall on the degree to which each is behaving in accord with the ethics of human development. This information is turned into a report (again, with anonymity protected) and given to leadership along with suggestions for using the feedback contained in the report to the benefit of the organization. This report can serve as a baseline, with the questionnaire readministered on a periodic basis for the purpose of tracking progress and identifying issues requiring additional work.

One of the primary goals of the training program is to help individuals build an ethical culture within their organizations. This means a culture that actively encourages and supports conduct in accord with the ethics of human development (or their facsimile), a culture committed to helping those within it realize their full potential as human beings. Implicit in the training program is the notion that one of the most important technologies any organization—or society, for that matter—can develop is one that encourages its members to think about and discuss their ethics. Such a technology, whatever form it takes, would be an attempt to provide individuals with the means for ensuring that the organizations that so dramatically affect them, the organizations wherein they work, study, and pursue their various interests, are organizations that are increasingly anchored to human logic.

The basic assumption behind the training program is that individuals and organizations that seek to honor the public trust must go beyond mere compliance with the law. They must also embrace, practice, and perhaps even teach—in whatever way is appropriate for them—the ethics that will lead to a better world.

THE THEATER OF CHANGE

One of the aims of this training experience is akin to the theater piece described by Wilshire at the beginning of Part V. Figuratively speaking, the training experience is an attempt "to raise the warehouse door," permitting participants to see the workplace—indeed, everyday life, the here and now—as the place wherein development occurs depending on how one chooses to behave. The workplace is not only a setting where we earn our livelihood but, like everyday life, also a theater wherein the forming of who we are as persons continues.

Habit and routine, so often a part of everyday work and in many cases necessary to it, can have a numbing effect. When coupled with the decision to go along with things as they are, avoid difficult issues and remain invisible, habit and routine can put us to sleep. The aim of training is to wake participants up to the theater in which they find themselves, to invite them to consider (or reconsider) their obligations to themselves and to their workplace (among other settings), and to give them practice in dealing with issues they may have avoided previously. In addition to presenting the ethics of human development, the aim of training is to help participants become aware of themselves as actors in an ongoing play—not cogs in a machine but individuals capable of consciously interacting with others and with organizational structures in ways that have developmental consequences. In other words, the aim is to further participants' awareness of their capacity for choice, to make them aware of the fact that they are already engaged in choosing among many possibilities—hour by hour, minute by minute—however much they may have denied or been unaware of this fact previously.

This is one of the reasons role-players are asked to rehearse their scripts in advance of training. Participants generally enjoy seeing colleagues and friends enact a scene no matter how much they may stumble over a script, lose their place, or fall out of character. But with rehearsal, the stumbling is minimized. Role-players have the opportunity to practice reading their parts aloud and giving them what life they can. They come to the training session ready and therefore create less distraction from the content of the scene. This rehearsed and more polished presentation gives seriousness to the scene, making its relevance harder to dismiss. It enhances the mirror the enacted scenes attempt to provide, giving participants less to distract them from the opportunity for self-reflection even as the effort continues throughout training to keep the setting informal and relaxed.

According to Wilshire, the term *theater* comes from the Greek word *theatron*, meaning "a place for seeing."[5] The training experience is an attempt to be such a place, a place where glimpses of the self can penetrate past participant defenses, giving them a sharpened view of themselves and, in that "seeing," an awareness they did not have previously. In other words, to see and, in that seeing, to objectify, permitting examination and additional perspective, and in this process, if one does not like what is seen, to consider other ways of behaving.

One additional goal of training comes by way of analogy from the world of horse racing. At some point in every race, if the possibility of winning is sensed, the jockey "asks" his mount to go for the win. This asking can come in many forms: a movement of the reins, vocal cues, the showing of the whip. But however it comes, jockeys refer to it as *the posing of the question*.[6] This is what the role-playing scenes and the training experience overall attempt to do—to help participants recognize when the question is being posed. With every enacted scene, participants are asked: Is this scene relevant to you? Are there situations like it that occur in your everyday life? How about this scene? And this scene? Are any of these situations occurring at work or at home? What do the various scenes have in common? The training experience, through the use of many examples, attempts to help participants recognize those situations wherein the question is posed, and then to help them see themselves as capable of behaving in other ways if to do so seems desirable. This ability to behave in other ways is enhanced through insight, through seeing (in the enacted scene) one's own ineptness or unconsciousness, and then enhanced further through risk-taking and practice (one's own or that of others).

It should be pointed out that although the ethics of human development guide the search for the ethical resolution to each scene, it is the group as a whole—their discussion, experimentation, and use of feedback—that reveals what the solution should look like if, in fact, a solution is to be found. The important thing is to enact the scene, determine whether or not it is relevant, discuss and enact possible solutions, and then to continue to do so, involving as many participants as are willing until the best of what the group can imagine is on display. The willingness to experiment is critical. Participants hopefully come to discover (through their own efforts or those of a stand-in) that behavior is mutable and that within the situation there is usually time to recognize what is occurring and therefore time to choose a preferred response, one that buys time if not resolution. If no solution is found through this process of enactment, discussion, and reenactment, then at the very least, participants leave the training with issues to mull over. A scene that looks like situations that arise at work or in everyday life is dissected with solution "fragments" now ready to be considered and recombined.

A MEANS FOR SELF-MAKING

Ultimately, the ethics of human development and the training program designed to teach them are about the making of the self, about ethics as human logic. It is certainly true that we are inevitably and necessarily made or authored by others—fathers and mothers, teachers and peers, the social and moral order into which we are born. And these authoring influences are indispensable, so much so that without them, we might never acquire the ability to take over the task of self-authoring at the point where these influences leave off. We might never realize that it is our duty to continue working on a self that, by definition, others cannot finish for us. (Hence, the reason and necessity for Ethic 11: "It is ethical to continue to grow as a person, to continue to increase your capacity to conduct yourself in accord with your ethics and principles; unethical to stop growing as a person.") The point is that as the authoring goes on, the self increasingly becomes the product of its own making, not only taking over the task of self-forming but taking responsibility for the self that has been made by others[7]—changing, undoing, modifying what others have shaped into being to the point that no one else, no other outside factor, is to be held responsible for who one is or how one behaves. Credit may be due to any number of influences, but blame is out of the equation. Increasingly, the individual, through his own efforts and having taken over the controls, has become a self-responsible agent. This is a tall order and extremely difficult, but nevertheless a way of characterizing the far end of the developmental continuum discussed in Part I.

In *Role Playing and Identity*, Wilshire quotes the philosopher G. H. Mead, who wrote, "The self arises in conduct."[8] We act our way to maturity by addressing the difficult situations that come our way. We learn from our mistakes, choosing and deciding and acting our way to a self that is socially responsible, able to join with others (or not join with others, as the case may be) in pursuit of interpersonal and social arrangements that are more creative and just. In other words, a person whose very nature is to act on behalf of and in accord with the largest of possible motives, something that both outlasts oneself and contributes to the good of others. That nature emerges out of the ethical resolution of many, many ethical dilemmas until it becomes second nature—indeed, one's primary nature—to address such moments as they arise with openness, compassion, love, and resolve. That is what is meant by self-authoring. Through the willed and successful addressing of self-forming dilemmas, large and small, there comes a generalization. Conduct that could not be imagined or, if imagined, had to be willed in the face of considerable inertia is now the new normal, the way in which one behaves generally, with far less effort, drama, or dividedness.

One additional aspect or by-product of the point just made: Self-making dilemmas, when met effectively, increase our belief in ourselves. They strengthen our willingness to persist despite the obstacles in front of us. A person cannot evolve without the willingness to persist. Arthur Schopenhauer, the nineteenth-century philosopher, defined the will as "the strong blind man who carries upon his shoulders the lame man who can see."[9] The training program prescribes a means by which this blind man may be exercised and strengthened so that what is envisioned by the self for the self may be approximated through conduct.

None of the above is emphasized in training, however, or rarely so. Rather, the emphasis in training is first, simply, that the more experience we have in dealing with the dilemmas of everyday life, the better we get at dealing with them. Practice and experience lead to improvement. Second, to successfully address the dilemmas that come our way is to feel on purpose, to feel engaged with issues that have meaning for us and that may matter beyond us. And third, as we proceed in our effort to ethically resolve the dilemmas that come our way, the self that begins to come into view is one we esteem, one we respect for its courage and willingness to behave in accord with espoused values. These are the benefits emphasized in training, but they are in line with the notion that through the ethical resolution of the dilemmas that come our way, comes the making and maturing of the self.

FEAR AND LONGING

When individuals who have attended the training program rate their satisfaction with their own performance and with the performance of the organization on the various ethics of human development measures, the items with which they are invariably least satisfied are: "eliminating escape and avoidance from the management of self and others," "the absence of procrastination," "acting decisively when the time to act has come," "providing feedback to others." Participants identify those items in which apprehension, anxiety, trepidation, or fear can interfere with performance.

The questionnaire is completed at the end of training. Participants understand the meaning of the questions they are answering. Their ratings suggest that the reason they sometimes do not behave in accord with the ethics of human development is because they are afraid to do so: afraid of what will happen, of the consequences that will follow, whatever those consequences might be. That is why training emphasizes the fact that ethics training—or at least an ethics training program anchored to human logic—is as much about the way in which we are governed by fear as it is about the ethics that should characterize our behavior.

When facing ethical dilemmas, we often feel pulled in opposite directions. On the one hand, we are pulled by our sense of duty to ourselves, and others. In this direction lies personal development, integration, and wholeness. On the other hand, there is the impulse to ignore, to escape, or to avoid; in this direction lies giving up, settling, giving in to the current holding pattern. "To be or not to be" remains the question throughout our lives, and with this question comes the concern that we will choose the latter and not the former—the concern that we may simply lack the courage, understanding, and/or skill necessary to sustain even one more step along the Yellow Brick Road, and that instead we will opt for withdrawal.

While the issue of fear is discussed throughout training, as a matter of practice no one is asked to do anything with which they are uncomfortable. Participants are asked to say their name, what they do in the organization, and to participate in some large group image theater exercises. Beyond that, however, there is only self-examination, privately answered workbook questions, and the witnessing and voluntary discussing of scripted scenes. Of course, there is always the invitation to participate, the invitation to take greater risks, to enact and resolve the dilemma in a given scene (the decision to do so a dilemma of its own). And it is pointed out that the risking of oneself in an effort to enact one's best ideas is rarely, if ever, a bad idea, especially in the protective context of training. At the very least, participation of that sort is a request for feedback and shaping. But it is something more, as well. To get out of one's chair and attempt to enact a role-playing solution before an audience of both friends and new acquaintances, and to do so on behalf of an inkling or a conviction or an ideal is nothing less than a "turning of the Fool loose." It is using the play within the play for the cultivation of that very capacity that is needed both in the organization and in life—namely, the willingness to risk acting the fool on behalf of the best of what one knows, knowing that it may not be sufficient or the best of what can be known. Without this willingness, there is no evolution of self or society. And though the effort to do this by a given participant may appear clumsy or half-baked, such efforts are, in a sense, selfless.[10] The individual stands in for others, modeling what it takes and in the process setting the occasion for the development of a culture that itself needs practice in supporting such behavior—practice at providing feedback and support for the very activity that will enliven it.

THE ROLE OF CULTURE

This leads to a consideration of the role of culture in supporting development and, as well, in countering inertia and fear. As indicated previously, we often feel caught between two forces when confronting an ethical or self-making dilemma. We feel caught between the desire for greater integration, what Wilshire called "the ontological need,"[11] and entropy, disintegration, perhaps even the self-destructiveness that hastens disintegration. Culture provides a framework of supports that can fend off disintegration; that binds us to one another in such a way as to hold off decay.[12] It shields us, offering protection and stability. This is a restating of the center of gravity discussion offered in Part IV. The cultural center of gravity holds us to a particular standard that serves as both restraint and safety net. It's true that those above the culture's established standard are sometimes slowed in their pursuit of still higher standards, but it is always possible to fall below the established standard. And should that happen, the center of gravity is there to draw one back, slowing the fall and offering time and support for the individual to collect herself. At the same time, to be above the established standard, to achieve and maintain an integrity not yet common in the culture, is one of the ways we serve others, helping to hold in place and perhaps even raise the existing standard.

There is yet another role culture can play in personal development. It is the role culture plays when used intentionally by individuals who recognize its power to affect change. Most of us are a part of several organizations and, thus, several cultures at any one time. By taking responsibility for the cultures of which we are a part, we use the power of culture to accelerate development. By choosing wisely the community in which we live (if that option exists); by choosing carefully our friendships, our workplace; by inserting ourselves into cultures that educate us, keep us fit, encourage us to contribute to others—cultures that require us to exercise our flexibility, our creativity, cultures comprised of those we admire and that, in turn, require the best of us—by these means we create a "funnel of becoming."[13] Our affiliations, whether to individuals or organizations, can provide support for the further integration and wholeness that is possible. The goal remains progress on the Yellow Brick Road. But the pursuit of that goal can include this additional stratagem, the conscious use of culture—of many cultures patchworked together—to draw, pull, funnel, and support, accelerating the emergence of a human being that is creative, playful, principled, and compassionate. This achievement, if it does occur, belongs to the individual who accomplishes it but also to culture and its power to transform and refine.

Remember, as the term is used here, culture can exist not only on a global, regional, and ethnic level but also in a neighborhood, a school, a classroom. A culture exists in every organization and workplace, in families, and even between two people. The emphasis here is on the pattern of exchange between people, the give-and-take, and the values that pattern of exchange expresses and supports, rather than on the language, arts, and traditions of a given group. The point is to seek out and insert oneself into a pattern of exchange that is growth-promoting; the conscious, intentional use of culture to help bring about personal development, the further refinement of the self, refinement meaning *soulful* in this context, not sophistication in the world of arts and letters.

THE MORAL CLIMAX

As early as the 1970s, Buckminster Fuller argued that humanity is facing its final exam. Utopia or oblivion is the way he put it, the explosions in population, knowledge, interdependency, and awareness having driven humanity to this point.[14] Human beings cannot turn around now without bumping into one another. We are connected by proximity, although not by proximity alone. The planet is wired. Even in the most remote villages there are satellite dishes and, with them, awareness of the events, lifestyles, and disparities that characterize our historical moment. Furthermore, this planetary web only continues to tighten—interpersonally, organizationally, and internationally—the result being that we just can't get away with wronging others as we used to. No longer is it as possible to "do unto others" without also "doing unto ourselves," to "win" at the expense of others without also experiencing some degree of loss. As game theorists say, we are in a non–zero sum game.[15]

To put it another way, we seem to be invited as never before by the potentially life-threatening and irreversible consequences of our actions to become more conscious, more responsible, more ethical, for our own sake if not for the sake of others. A more mature version of ourselves would appear to be needed, a version capable of considering the long-term consequences of actions and thus of aligning our actions with what is likely to work for more of us—ideally, for all of us—over the long run.

The question that resides at the heart of Fuller's "final exam" (and at the heart of this book) is among the most fundamental questions that can be asked: Who are we? What are we? From the point of view of this book, the answer is: *We are the effects we have on others.*[16] We may be more than that, but we are at least that. And while it is true that we can never know the exact or full effect we have on others, still, with detachment from our need for self-protective conclusions, we nevertheless can see that we are producing effects through our involvements with others and with the physical and biological environment—effects that may or may not be short-lived, that flow into and merge with the effects of others, but effects nonetheless. As individuals who wish to evolve, it is our job to see these effects, to discern them however they trace through, contribute to, and condition the experience and development of others. For in the seeing of these effects, we see ourselves. In our effects on others and on the physical and biological environment, we find the looking glass, the mirror; and with it, what Becker meant when he said, "People create the reality they need in order to discover themselves." For there in the mirror we discover who we are, the current version of what we are. And again, if what is reflected can be seen with a minimum of self-protective rationalization, then a pivotal dilemma can arise—indeed, will arise if what is seen is not what we imagined for ourselves back when we thought calmly about what it was we wanted to become.

Such a moment in a person's life constitutes a moral climax—a coming face-to-face with a self that is so inconsistent with our values that we must either turn away from self-reflection and witnessing altogether (a choice that some people do indeed make) or, at last, change course. It is a pivotal moment in a person's life. And what Fuller argued is that such a moment now exists for humankind.

In their book *The Lessons of History*, Will and Ariel Durant wrote, "The only real revolution is in the enlightenment of the mind and the improvement of character, the only real emancipation is individual, and the only real revolutionists are philosophers and saints."[17] At its core, the focus of this book—and the training program discussed above—is on the individual, on the enlightenment of the mind and the improvement of character through conduct in accord with the ethics of human development. The focus is on the development of individuals who can effectively and ethically navigate the morality play that is life on this planet. The liberation that is both sought and required is from small-mindedness, from the frustrations and self-destructiveness of unruly and unconscious motivations, and from the sense of alienation and cutoffness that separate us from ourselves and others. This is not a book or a program that makes us philosophers or saints. It is, however, a book and program about self-development and social change, about assisting in the revolution of which the Durants wrote.

Schumacher suggested that we need to see the world in a new light, "as a place where the things modern man continuously talks about and always fails to accomplish can actually be done."[18] The Earth is generous, he argued, and there is no reason for anyone to live in misery. Like Fuller, Schumacher believed that the know-how to make the world work for everyone exists and that more know-how is being developed daily. For Schumacher, Fuller's "network of unstable holding patterns held in place by ignorance and fear" is the ethical dilemma of our time.

The approach taken in this book calls for the conscious pursuit of levels of being and modes of conduct always above our own, with progress on the Yellow Brick Road held as the fundamental and guiding value. An essential part of the answer to Schumacher's and Fuller's moral dilemma resides in the development of the conscious and ethical self. With that development, and offering the measure of it, come decisions and actions that leverage the future in humanity's favor—decisions and actions that, by degree, are driven less by ignorance and fear and more by reason, vision, and love; decisions made by individuals who can recognize an ethical/self-forming dilemma when it presents itself and who can respond with more of humanity's welfare, life itself, in mind. These individuals have achieved a remarkable degree of self-mastery and with it a profound sense of life's possibility. They have realized and manifested through their actions one of the most important of all inherent possibilities: the ability to become and remain (as Wilshire put it) "aware, interpreting and free,"[19] valuing and serving the emergence of that same ability in others. This so that life can increasingly be valued first among competing concerns. And this so that life, the nature of being itself, can realize whatever inherent possibility resides within it.

SUMMARY

There are many legitimate approaches to addressing the dilemmas facing modern man. Here the focus is on the self-change that is invariably social change; the self-change that is certain to strengthen what Robert Wright calls "the fabric of mutual benefit."[20] The individual who pursues his maturity through conduct in accord with the ethics of human development cannot help but positively impact the organizations of which he is a part. The organization committed to building within itself an ethical culture cannot help but affect the development of its members. And this effort on the part of both inevitably affects the larger community. After all, a community is simply a very large organization, made up of hundreds or even thousands of smaller organizations (not to mention the families that comprise it). How many of these smaller organizations must be actively engaged in building ethical cultures within themselves—cultures anchored to human logic—before the larger community begins to benefit from their effort? A few hundred businesses? A few dozen corporations? The schools? Local governmental and volunteer agencies? How can the training and active support of human development at these various levels not spill over and be felt by the larger community? This is one way for communities to transform themselves. The focus is on the individual, on the complete energizing of our capacities as selves or persons. The unit of change, however, is twofold: both individual and organizational. As both benefit, so too does the larger community, since the larger community can only be as prosperous and as creative, as ecologically sane and life-embracing, as the character of its citizens and their organizations permit.

Afterword

"Justice, in the ethical sense, is giving to every [person] the indispensable conditions of self-realization."[1]

—Wilbur Marshall Urban
Fundamentals of Ethics

The preface of this book suggested that life can be viewed in any number of ways, but that here, it would be viewed as a morality play. What has been offered in the intervening pages is a code of ethics for helping to ensure that the play continues. It is a code that matures us and makes our organizations more effective and humane; a code, therefore, that reduces the likelihood that we will self-destruct. Such a code is needed if we are to have any hope of discovering what the play is about. And in the end, that is the question on our minds: What is this play about?

The answer, of course, is that we do not know. Our current level of understanding and our current level of development do not permit us an answer. It is obvious, however, that unless we stick around, we will never know the answer. Humanity must continue, through time and down the Yellow Brick Road, in order to grasp the storyline, the larger narrative—grasp and, if need be, shape, giving it a direction that ensures not only survival but also joy and fulfillment. That is the ultimate function of the ethics of human development: to help shape the narrative. That is what we are doing whenever we behave in accord with the ethics of human development or ethically resolve our everyday dilemmas. We are shaping the narrative, the narrative of self, workplace, and society, and so, to a degree, the narrative of the play itself.

Two assumptions underlie this book. First, we want the fulfillment of our potential, the full realization of inherent possibilities. Second, ethical conduct facilitates the emergence of that potential, and provides evidence of it. Along the way, a third assumption was added: It is not madness to have utopian ideals. The non–zero sum game, the world working for everyone (as Buckminster Fuller put it), the opportunity for all people to travel the Yellow Brick Road—these are conceptualizations or goals humanity rejects at its peril. And while it is hard to imagine how such goals can be reached, the cause is presumably served if we can establish a link between these goals and the life of the self in the midst of its everyday travails. That has been the background purpose of this book: to provide that link, to show that the ethics of human development and the resolution of our everyday dilemmas aim us in the direction of an ideal, a self-realization that necessarily strengthens the fabric of mutual regard. It is true that while some gains resulting from our efforts may be too small to measure or even notice, others are not, as the dilemmas we face come in all sizes. The cumulative effect of our effort, however, gives evidence of the fact that we are not indifferent to our own future or to the future of life in general, and that we are capable of behaving with the realization of inherent possibilities and long-run ideals in mind.

Notes

Preface

[1] Durant, Will. *The Mansions of Philosophy*. Garden City, NY: Garden City Publishing Co., 1929, p. 20.

[2] My apologies to the commentator in question. I do not have his name and this is not an exact quote, rather the spirit of what I remember him saying. The comment was made during a discussion on the MacNeil/Lehrer PBS NewsHour following Roger's death.

[3] Throughout this book, the use of the term "self" is shorthand for person or individual: "the development of the self" synonymous with "the development of the person," "selfhood" synonymous with "personhood".

[4] I first became aware of "ethics as human logic" via a quote from Edwin M. Epstein of the Walter A. Haas School of Business at the University of California–Berkeley, along the lines of: "The Japanese word for ethics, *rinri*, translates roughly as 'human logic' or the 'way of being human.'" Later I discovered Watsuji Tetsuro's *Rinrigaku* (*Ethics in Japan*), translated by Yamamoto Seisaku and Robert E. Carter, published by State University of New York Press, Albany, 1996. As Tetsuro puts it, ethics are "the way human beings truly become human beings" (p. 22).

[5] Whitman, Walt. From "Carol of Words" in *Leaves of Grass*. Philadelphia: David McKay, 1900, p. 219.

[6] To speak of enlightenment is tricky business. I do not mean the enlightenment of the mystic, the nondual consciousness that comes suddenly or perhaps after years of meditative practice. Nor do I mean the enlightenment of the Buddhist that marks an awakening to ultimate truth. Rather, I mean a kind of behavioral enlightenment, the capacity to engage in behavior that reflects a concern for one's own development as well as an ever-wider concern for the wellbeing and development of others.

[7] Becker, Ernest. *The Denial of Death*. New York: The Free Press, 1973, p. 158.

Part I—*Human Development and the Yellow Brick Road*

1 Schumacher, E. F. *A Guide for the Perplexed*. New York: Harper & Row, 1977, p. 132.

2 Savory, Allan. *Holistic Resource Management*. Covelo, CA: Island Press, 1988, p. 398. The Irish philosopher John O'Donohue expresses this same notion poetically in his book *Beauty: The Invisible Embrace* (New York: Harper Perennial, 2005, p. 47): "There is a wonderful urgency within things to realize the dream of their individual fulfillment; nothing is neutral, everything is on its way."

3 See the work of John David Garcia, in particular *The Moral Society: A Rational Alternative to Death* (New York: The Julian Press, 1971) and *Creative Transformation: A Practical Guide for Maximizing Creativity* (Eugene, OR: Noetic Press and Ardmore, PA: Whitmore Publishing Company, 1991). Garcia's work in general and, in particular, his identification of the ethics required for creative and evolutionary advance, along with his analysis of the relationship of ethics to bureaucracy, are brilliant accomplishments to which this book owes a great deal.

4 The "Yellow Brick Road" is a key element in L. Frank Baum's novel *The Wizard of Oz*. Dorothy, Baum's central character, must travel the Yellow Brick Road if she has any hope of returning to her beloved home. Another use of the Yellow Brick Road can be found in Norman Spinrad's remarkable novel *Child of Fortune* (New York: Bantam Books, 1985). See for example p. xi: "But all too many adolescents in all too many cultures never passed through Chaos at all. They were born, they were acculturated, they were schooled, they took up their adult stations in life, passed through an ill-defined period of mid-life angst, resigned themselves to old age, and died, without ever walking the Yellow Brick Road, indeed without ever understanding what it was they had missed in their lives."

5 Many such maps or systems depicting the stages of human development exist. See for example Schumacher (*A Guide for the Perplexed*); Ken Wilber (*Sex, Ecology and Spirituality: The Spirit of Evolution*, and in particular, *Integral Psychology*, in which Wilber presents and compares many developmental systems); Robert Kegan *(The Evolving Self);* and Timothy Leary (*Exo-Psychology*). The system presented here was developed in 1983. It is from this system—working with it and using it as a backdrop—that this book, and the ethics of human development in particular, evolved. As for the origin of this system, I first developed the five levels (i.e., No Mind, Hive Mind, etc.) and began exploring ways of making that sequence useful as a way of describing human development. It was during that time that I read *The Mirror and the Lamp*, in which M. H. Abrams argues that the metaphor for the mind from Plato's time to the time of the Romantic poets was the mirror, at which point

it became the lamp. I therefore aligned the mirror with Hive Mind and the lamp with Poetic Mind, and began asking the questions that allowed me to flesh out the schematic. The schematic was completed in short order except for two entries. It was my colleague Dan Daly, PhD, who suggested that I use the eagle for Heroic Mind and the dolphin for Poetic Mind.

6 This is a critical measure of society at all points, and an indictment of society when the higher levels are denied or prevented altogether in some way.

7 See the work of Owen Barfield, i.e., *The Rediscovery of Meaning and other Essays* (Middleton, CT: Wesleyan University Press, 1977) and *Saving the Appearances: A Study of Idolatry* (New York: Harcourt Brace Jovanovich, 1965).

8 This level could readily be labeled "Moral Mind," "Ethical Mind," "Adult Mind," "Whole Mind," "Integral Mind," or "Integrated Mind." When the schematic was first developed, it was labeled "Never Mind," as in "never mind all that would otherwise distract you from behaving in accord with this level's standard of conduct."

9 Eckart Tolle makes this point in his books *The Power of Now* (Novato, CA: New World Library, 1999) and *A New Earth: Awakening to Your Life's Purpose* (New York: Penguin Group, 2006).

10 This is Ken Wilber's "center of gravity" concept (discussed in Part IV) applied to the self. See *A Brief History of Everything* (Boston & London: Shambhala Publications, 1996, p. 139).

11 This quote is found in a book entitled *Child* edited by Helen Handley and Andra Samelson (New York: Pushcart Press, 1988, p. 66) containing quotations from a variety of authors on the nature and experience of childhood.

12 See *The Illuminated Rumi*, translations and commentary by Coleman Barks (New York: Broadway Books, 1997, p. 95).

13 One additional point: Even if one is unaware of the way in which the pursuit of mastery in one's work serves as a metaphor, still there is a contribution made whenever and wherever mastery occurs. The environment is enriched by it, by an event or a product or a transaction that raises the overall standard present in the environment. We are called/inspired to the higher reaches of our own development (in part, at least) by the excellence we see in others, by their deeds, their great works, their way of being in the world. That is why great work, regardless of profession, is almost always a community service. It builds an environment that calls those in it to a higher standard, and it does so by example. Whenever we respond to this call, or are inspired by others to address our own performance, we are responding to the needs of

our higher nature and attempting, however erringly, to narrow the distance between what we can accomplish now and what we might accomplish if the integrating pull of that higher nature is to have its way. The most inspiring mastery, as suggested in the text, is the mastery of the self. But some degree of self-mastery is involved whenever outstanding contributions are made, and it is likely that it is the witnessing of this self-mastery, as much as the achievement it makes possible, that inspires our admiration and moves us to explore our own inherent possibilities.

14 Wilber, *Integral Psychology*, pp. 47–53; Wilber, *Sex, Ecology, Spirituality*, pp. 51–54.

15 Referring to the work of Don Beck/Spiral Dynamics, this is what Wilber calls "the Prime Directive, not preferential treatment of any one level" (*Integral Psychology*, p. 232). The problem, according to Wilber and others (*Integral Psychology*, pp. 230–32), is that prior to Level Five (excluding Level One), each level (or the mindset associated with each level) considers itself to have "arrived" and experiences the motives and worldview of other levels as error, threat, or both. The tension or battle between these levels of mind is played out on the evolutionary stage as each level views the others with varying degrees of fear, suspicion, and disdain. Only with maturity comes perspective, a compassion that allows each level its place within a developmental sequence. And though the other levels may view Level V with the same suspicion/disdain that they view one another, those who achieve Level V have one key motivational advantage: They know that their growth and continuing maturation depends in part on the development they are able to support in others. For a literary expression of this point, see Norman Spinrad's *Child of Fortune*, in which he writes: "For while the subject of my sanity at any stage of the tale and the sequence in which my consciousness revolved was to be a matter of endless learned debate by Healers and mages far better versed in the scientific lore than I, in the entirely amateur opinion of the subject in question, my full *humanity* was restored when I accepted responsibility, however reluctantly, for preserving the humanity of others," (p. 350). See also Colin Wilson's *Poetry and Mysticism* (San Francisco: City Lights Books, 1969, p. 201): "The real conflict in [human beings] is not between 'body' and 'spirit,' but between different levels of mind."

16 Carse, James. *Finite and Infinite Games*. New York: Ballantine Books, 1986, p. 144.

Part II—*Human Logic and the Ethics of Human Development*

1 Urban, Wilbur Marshall. *Fundamentals of Ethics*. New York: Henry Holt and Company, 1939, p. 118.

2 See preface, note 3.

3 Garcia, *Creative Transformation.*

4 Ibid., p. 324.

5 Both Ethic 2: The Open-Mindedness Ethic and Ethic 3: The Deliberate Action Ethic draw heavily on the work of John David Garcia. See for example *The Moral Society: A Rational Alternative to Death* (New York: The Julian Press, 1971, p. 1): "In the end, a person who is honest with himself always has doubts . . ." Garcia writes: "1) It is unethical to be certain; 2) it is ethical to doubt; and 3) inaction is unethical." In *Creative Transformation: A Practical Guide for Maximizing Creativity* (Eugene, OR: Noetic Press and Ardmore, PA: Whitmore Publishing Company, 1991), Garcia returns to this point (p. 306): "Our models of nature cannot evolve unless we doubt their validity." In *The Moral Society* (p. 140), Garcia adds a corollary to this argument: "It is unethical to give up hope because it is unethical to be certain."

6 This is a point made over and over again in the works of Wilber. See for example *Sex, Ecology, Spirituality: The Spirit of Evolution* (London & Boston: Shambhala Publications, 1995).

7 Garcia, *The Moral Society*, p. 1: "The problem each person must solve for himself is how to act ethically when the future outcome of every act is uncertain."

8 Again, Garcia offers guidance: "We should try to avoid any act which might result in irreversible damage if our judgment is in error, although it is better to act decisively than not to act at all." *Creative Transformation,* p. 152.

9 Boal, Augusto. *Games for Actors and Non-Actors*. New York: Routledge, Chapman and Hall, 1992, p. xxv.

10 Throughout both *The Moral Society* and *Creative Transformation*, Garcia emphasizes the importance of giving and receiving feedback. In *The Moral Society* (p. 38), he writes: "Deliberate destruction of feedback is always immoral." In *Creative Transformation* (p. 255): "The great challenge is to give negative feedback with love and humility and not with anger and arrogance."

11 Garcia, *The Moral Society*, p. 31.

12 As an aside, it is only through the inviting of feedback—the openness to and welcoming of feedback—that we realize that feedback is ever-present, that there is a continuous feedback loop between self and world. And though much of the feedback we receive is subtle and easily missed when one is in a "noisy" or distracted state of mind, it is there and helpful beyond measure—the continuous conversation, rapport, or dialogue between self and world that helps one define and perhaps expand the sense of self.

[13] Garcia, *Creative Transformation,* p. 270: "When we love someone we must give them clear and unavoidable negative feedback when they are destructive, recognizing that they may be right and that we may be in error. If they refuse this feedback or its intent, then their own fear will drive them away from us."

[14] Kegan, Robert, and Lahey, Lisa Laskow. *How the Way We Talk Can Change the Way We Work.* San Francisco: Jossey-Bass, 2001, p. 101. Kegan and Leskow write (p. 99): "If we characterize people, even if we do so quite positively, we actually engage—however unintentionally—in the rather presumptuous activity of entitling ourselves to say who and how the other is. We entitle ourselves to confer upon people the sources of their worthiness."

[15] Ibid, p. 101: "This is not what we mean by the language of ongoing regard. Ongoing regard is not about praising, stroking, or positively defining a person to herself or to others. We say again: it is about enhancing the quality of a precious kind of information. It is about informing the person about our experience of him or her."

[16] Peck, M. Scott. *The Road Less Traveled.* New York: Simon and Schuster, 1978, pp. 62-63.

[17] Will Schultz was one of the founders of the human potential movement. I was unable to find in my notes the exact reference for this quote, only that it should be attributed to Schultz.

[18] The Enron debacle is a case in point. In that situation, the truth was withheld for self-serving ends, withheld so a few could escape the collapsing edifice with their gains intact while others, excluded from the truth, were certain to lose everything. This caused outrage where before there had been trust. The understandable response to such a situation is an increase in policing, an increase in the network of regulations that ensure accountability so that all players—not just the few—are protected against one group taking advantage of another. This increase in regulation may be healthy, it may in fact be what is needed, but it illustrates what happens when the trust built up through truth-telling (as well as through ethical performance in general) is broken. The environment becomes more complex, and the simplicity and ease of navigation that were possible when trust prevailed is reduced.

[19] Lao Tsu. *The Tao Te Ching*. New York: Vintage Books, 1989, p. 65.

[20] Tolle, Eckhart. *The Power of Now.* Novato, CA: New World Library, 1999, p. 181.

[21] Ethic 7 raises a complicated and delicate issue; namely, the presumption of choice. We have and make choices and are free to do so. We are not the victims we sometimes portray ourselves to be.

But is that so: We make choices and are free to do so? It is certainly the case that our histories obviously and dramatically affect the choices we make. It might even be accurate to say that our histories determine the choices we make, a statement that undercuts the notion of free choice altogether. We are not outside the web of cause and effect; we are within it, a part of it, everyone acting in accord with the causes that impinge upon them. Where is the freedom in a system in which actions flow necessarily from what has preceded them?

And yet, as is discussed in the body of the text, our histories are learning histories. We learn from our experience. We learn to observe, to engage in forethought, to think about what will happen if we do this or that. We become conscious. And as we become conscious, options appear. At some point, it seems natural and appropriate to say that we have choices. Appropriate, also, to say that we have responsibility for the choices we make.

Is this illusion? Does the complexity of our learning history prevent us from seeing the determinism that continues to operate? Perhaps. In fact it may not be possible to dispense with that possibility. However, what is presumed here is this: To develop and mature is to experience a shift in the locus of control from past conditioning to a conscious, deliberative, and aware self. This is a gradual shift brought about by the consequences of past acts, consequences that encourage us to pay attention, to think for ourselves, to consider the likely consequences of our future acts. We learn to pause, to reflect, to interrupt what were previously automatic chains of behavior with decisions to proceed or not to proceed. And with those learned skills, we become self-directing. We hold ourselves responsible for the choices we make, insisting that we learn from our mistakes—insisting, as well, that ethic, principle, goal, or vision govern our choices, not the restraints of past conditioning.

There are victims in this world, of course; far, far too many individuals who lack options and/or who did not in any meaningful sense choose or help create the situation in which they find themselves. And there are individuals whose learning histories are so distorted or incomplete that in the face of alternative options, they continue to choose the self-destructive. All of this is true, and true perhaps for all of us to some degree. The point here, however, is that it is possible to learn not to make victims of ourselves, not to make choices that are self-destructive; possible to acquire a learning history that supports the pursuit of personal development (as defined in Part I).

So, with Ethic 7, there is a slight of mind required: Apply Ethic 7 to yourself, but give others a wide berth. Assume that you have choice, that you are self-directing, that you are free to choose as you will. With that assumption, you push past unwarranted excuses and put yourself in a position to explore and perhaps expand the limits of your creativity. At the same time, recognize that the capacity for choice and self-direction is acquired, the result of a learning history that others may have yet to experience.

With that said, it is important to add that conduct in accord with the ethics of human development is one means for acquiring the learning history just discussed and for delivering that history to others. In fact, in many respects that is the purpose of the ethics of human development: to provide the experience that educates, matures, and enlightens, increasing in the process freedom from the constraints of past conditioning and, so, the capacity to choose in accord with principle and enlightened self-interest.

22 Garcia, *The Moral Society*, p. 13: "Each player [in the Game of Life] must assume that he has free will and is totally responsible for his actions." And p. 17: "Man is no longer forced to play the Game of Life. He must now play it deliberately." In *Creative Transformation* (p. 159), Garcia writes: "Rules for the Game of Life: 1. Each player must assume that he or she always has free will and is totally responsible for all of his or her acts and whatever happens to him or her." And pp. 257–58: "In this belief, which I call the 'victim paradigm,' the persons are denying their free will . . . There is nothing more destructive that persons can do to themselves." Also, see Urban in *Fundamentals of Ethics* (p. 159): "The life of every man is a continuous process of choice. Even the refusal to choose, as William James was fond of pointing out, is itself a form of choice. No one can escape this fundamental character of human life, for it lies in the very nature of the life process itself." And p. 394: "The moral life is a continuous process of choice—of choice of one value over another and of choice of acts as leading to the realization of the chosen values. The question immediately arises whether this choice is real or only apparent, whether the will is free or actually determined. When the philosopher thinks things out, he cannot avoid the conclusion that if the moral life is to have any meaning at all, freedom of the will must be real." And p. 360: "For the [scientist] it seems, for instance, that for the universe to be rational it must be determined, and so the scientist seeks to find law and determinism in it. For morality, on the other hand, a rational universe must be one in which freedom is possible, so the moral philosopher seeks to find freedom in it. There is no real reason why one procedure should be 'rationalization' in the bad sense any more than the other. The philosopher at least refuses to start with either prejudice. Perhaps when he thinks things through, he will find both positions to have their element of truth. This at least is the possibility with which the philosopher starts. It is possible that it is also the conclusion to which he will finally come."

23 Berger, Peter. *Invitation to Sociology: A Humanistic Perspective*. Garden City, NY: Doubleday & Co., 1963, p. 143.

24 Miller, L. Keith. University of Kansas. Personal communication.

25 Schumacher, E. F. *Small is Beautiful: Economics As If People Mattered*. New York: Harper & Row Publishers, 1973. Also, see Schumacher's essay entitled, "Buddhist

Economics". Parabola, Vol. 16, No. 1, Spring 1991: "It is clear, therefore, that Buddhist economics must be very different from the economics of modern materialism, since the Buddhist sees the essence of civilization not in a multiplication of wants but in the purification of human character. Character, at the same time, is formed primarily by a man's work. And work, properly conducted in conditions of human dignity and freedom, blesses those who do it and equally their products."

26 Garcia, *The Moral Society*, p. 37: "To be ethical means that a person will correct his mistakes when they are perceived and that he will not deliberately blind himself to them." See also Urban (*Fundamentals of Ethics*, p. 377) for another way of discussing the notion of conscious mistakes: "This is what ordinary people mean when they say that, although men may differ as to what things are right or wrong, no one ever thinks that it is right to do wrong or wrong to do right."

27 From an interview with Chuck Berry in *Hail, Hail, Rock & Roll*, a documentary film by director Taylor Hackford, 1987.

28 There are, of course, what might be considered positive addictions such as exercise, meditation, one's creative activity, activities that do not make us weaker but in fact strengthen us. This is the point that physician William Glasser makes in his book, *Positive Addiction*. New York: Harper & Row, Publishers, 1976. Bruce Wilshire makes a similar point in *Wild Hunger: The Primal Roots of Modern Addiction*. New York: Rowman & Littlefield Publishers, 1998. Wilshire writes (pp. 98-99): " . . . the withdrawal symptom criterion includes within the class of addictive behaviors those that should not be called that at all. Take ardent mountain climbing or an all-absorbing artistic career or serious playing of any sort. Very difficult it is to give these up, and if they were to be withdrawn, distress would occur." Even so, Wilshire points out, these activities feed us, giving us more than they take away. The addiction discussed in the text, however, is the addiction arrived at primarily through conscious mistakes, through the conscious choosing of the option that at some level is recognized as self-destructive. This is the addiction that takes away more than it gives, weakening the capacity for choice while also narrowing the range of options from which one might choose.

29 Carey, Ken. Tape presentation of his book *The Third Millennium: Living in the Posthistoric Posthistoric World*. New York: HarperCollins, 1991.

30 Platt, John R. "Social Traps." In *American Psychologist*, Vol. 28, No. 8, August 1973, pp. 641–51.

31 Hardin, Garrett. "The Tragedy of the Commons." In *Science*, Vol. 162, 1968, pp. 1,243–48.

[32] Platt, "Social Traps," p. 643.

[33] Rachlin, Howard, and Green, Leonard. "Commitment, Choice and Self-Control." In the *Journal of the Experimental Analysis of Behavior*, Vol. 17, 1972, pp. 15–22.

[34] Hardin, Garrett. *Exploring New Ethics for Survival: The Voyage of the Spaceship Beagle*. New York: Viking Press, 1972, pp. 18–19.

[35] Platt, "Social Traps," p. 650.

[36] Hardin, *Exploring New Ethics for Survival*, pp. 77–87.

[37] See Ostrom, Elinor. *Governing the Commons: The Evolution of Institutions for Collective Action*. Cambridge, United Kingdom: Cambridge University Press, 2003. Ostrom surveys a variety of models and methods utilized by both organizations and individuals to voluntarily manage shared resources.

[38] The work of psychologist Lawrence Kohlberg focused on moral development and on what he considered the stages of moral development; see L. Kohlberg, "Moral Development and Identification," in *Yearbook*, National Society for the Study of Education, 1962. See also Arthur J. Deikman's *The Observing Self: Mysticism and Psychotherapy* (Boston: Beacon Press, 1982, pp. 85–89). Kohlberg argued that individuals pass through a sequence of moral development stages: the egocentric stage, for example, in which self-identity extends to the boundary of the skin and not much further, where the focus of moral concern is on "my needs," "my wishes," "my survival"; the ethnocentric stage, in which self-identity expands to include one's clan, tribe, community, or nation, with the focus of moral concern expanded to include "my clan's needs, wishes, and requirements"; and the worldcentric stage, in which self-identity expands to all people everywhere, the focus of the individual's concern now on what is needed in order for all people to survive and prosper. Conduct, he argued, aligns with the stage at which the individual finds herself, a point frequently made in the writings of Ken Wilber. Wilber notes that society would be wise to organize with this fact in mind, building in the supports that will help ensure conduct that does not harm society while at the same time allowing the individual the time needed to develop and mature. This same point is recognized by the field known as applied behavior analysis, though the notion of "stages as internal, unfolding structures" would be discarded in favor simply of an analysis of what the individual can and cannot do. If the desired behavior is absent (in this case, for example, behavior consistent with worldcentric concerns), then the "contingencies of reinforcement" present in the environment are rearranged in order to shape and maintain the desired behavior until the individual is able to maintain the behavior on her own. The purpose of applied behavior analysis is, in part, to help individuals acquire the self-control

that will allow them to behave in accord with their long-term desired ends (L. Keith Miller, University of Kansas, personal communication).

[39] For more on the idea of the Wind Harp, see Barfield, *The Rediscovery of Meaning*, pp. 65–78.

[40] Miller, Alice. *The Drama of the Gifted Child*. New York: Basic Books, 1981.

[41] Garcia, *Creative Transformation*, as well as his online publications at www. see.org/ garcia/.

[42] Bartley III, W.W. *Werner Erhard, The Transformation of a Man: The Founding of est*. New York: Clarkson N. Potter, 1978, p. 20.

[43] This ethic, as with others already mentioned, owes much to the writings of Garcia. This point in particular—that we have an ethical requirement to share our gift with at least one other person for their benefit—is Garcia's.

[44] Fuller, Buckminster. "The Fifty Year Experiment," an audio tape published by New Dimensions, San Francisco, 1982. This is a slight modification in the wording of Fuller's statement.

[45] Hyde, Lewis. *The Gift: Imagination and the Erotic Life of Property*. New York: Vintage Books, 1983, pp. 35–39.

[46] Ibid, pp. 38–39, 74–75, 78, 153, 194.

[47] Ibid, p. 25.

[48] Fuller, Buckminster. *Cosmography: A Posthumous Scenario for the Future of Humanity*. New York: Macmillan Publishing Co., 1992, p. 117.

Part III—*Dilemmas from Work and Everyday Life*

[1] *Sports Night*, a television series that aired from 1998 to 2000, created by Aaron Sorkin. See www.imdb.com/title/tt0165961/. The particular *Sports Night* episode referred to here was entitled "The Six Southern Gentlemen from Tennessee."

[2] To define the self is a rather large task. In an article entitled, "Perspectives on Selfhood", psychologist M. Brewster Smith discussed the nature of selfhood, what it is and how it might be acquired. Concerning its features, Smith writes: "So: Selfhood involves being *self-aware* or *reflective; being* or *having* a body . . .; somehow taking into account the *boundaries of selfhood* at birth and death and feeling a *continuity of identity* in between; placing oneself in a *generational sequence and network of*

other connected selves as forebears and descendants and relatives; being in partial *communication and communion with other contemporary selves* while experiencing an irreducible *separateness of experience and identity;* engaging in joint and individual *enterprises* in the world with some degree of *forethought and afterthought* (not just "behaving"); guiding what one does and appraising what one has done at least partly through *reflection* on one's performance; feeling *responsible,* at least sometimes, for one's actions and holding others responsible for theirs." *American Psychologist,* 1978, *33,* 1053-1063. The aspect of selfhood discussed in the text addresses only a portion of what Smith suggests should be taken into consideration when defining the self. It is those aspects, however, that involve self-awareness, self-review, the continuity of identity, and the holding of oneself responsible for one's actions.

3 Deikman, *The Observing Self.*

4 Ibid., pp. 94–96.

5 Psychologist Steven Hayes argues that through the acquisition of language, the observing self is made as the individual learns to distinguish between I/you, here/there, and now/then. As Hayes points out, *I*, *here*, and *now* characterize (or are true for) all observations made throughout an individual's lifetime. In that sense, writes Hayes, "the 'I' is boundless (or is experienced as such)"; it is therefore not bounded by time or space since the "I" is always present whenever and wherever observations occur. See Steven C. Hayes's *Get Out of Your Mind & Into Your Life: The New Acceptance & Commitment Therapy* (Oakland, CA: New Harbinger Publications, 2005, pp. 94–95).

6 In his book, *The Illusion of Technique* (New York: Anchor Books, 1973, p.322) William Barrett addresses the issue of being and becoming, or Being and doing, as he puts it. His conclusion: "The truth of human life must perpetually lie in the tension between Being and doing. We can never resolve the question exclusively in favor of one or the other side. All our doing must take place within the context of Being, with its mystery present and alive to us. Otherwise we are simply scurrying around aimlessly in the mazes of our own contrivances. On the other hand, to seek absorption in Being, as an escape from the tasks of ordinary life, can only lead to quiescence and boring repletion. Man is the creature who must live in perpetual tension between these opposites. He is their tension and copresence."

7 Wilshire, Bruce. *Role Playing and Identity: The Limits of Theatre as Metaphor.* Bloomington, IN: Indiana University Press, pp. xiii, 14, 272.

8 Deikman, *The Observing Self*, pp. 10, 172.

9 From "Don Juan in Hell," Act III from *Man and Superman* by George Bernard Shaw; see www.bigeye.com/donjuan.htm.

10 Hurston, Zora Neale. *Their Eyes Were Watching God*. New York: HarperCollins Publishers, 1990, pp. 8–9.

11 Fuller, *Cosmography*, p. 29.

12 Schumacher, *A Guide for the Perplexed*, p. 83.

13 Whitman's epic poem *Leaves of Grass* is both exercise and celebration of this point, the moral imagination expanded until self-identity includes all people in all ways of life. "In all people I see myself—none more, and not one a barleycorn less; / And the good or bad I say of myself, I say of them." *Leaves of Grass*, Mineola, NY: Dover Publications, 2007, p. 35.

14 This scene was inspired by—and is a slight modification of—a scene from *The West Wing*, a television series that aired from 1999 to 2006), created by Aaron Sorkin. See http://en.wikipedia.org/wiki/The_West_Wing.

15 See the works of Ken Keyes Jr., in particular *Handbook of Higher Consciousness*, Berkeley, CA: Living Love Center, 1975.

16 Philosopher Owen Barfield wrote extensively about the imagination and its role in the pursuit of meaning and greater self-awareness. See for example *Poetic Diction: A Study of Meaning* (Middleton, CT: Wesleyan University Press, 1971), and *Romanticism Comes of Age* (Middleton, CT: Wesleyan University Press, 1966).

Part IV—*The Ideas with Which We See*

1 Schumacher, *A Guide for the Perplexed*, p. 72.

2 This is a point that Wilber makes over and over in his work, as does Garcia.

3 In this connection, I want to acknowledge the work of Maria Nemeth, PhD. See *Mastering Life's Energies: Simple Steps to a Luminous Life at Work and Play* (Novato, CA: New World Library, 2007).

4 Schumacher, *A Guide for the Perplexed*, pp. 70–79.

5 By transcending history, I do not mean something magical, done by sleight of hand. Rather, I mean one or more of the following: seeing one's history in a new light; that is, emphasizing and deemphasizing certain elements, themes, and events until that history aligns with or seems to lead to the conduct one is pursuing in the present. "It is

the genius in us," wrote James Carse (*Finite and Infinite Games*, p. 87), "who knows that the past is most definitely past, and therefore not forever sealed but forever open to creative reinterpretation." This process of creatively reinterpreting the past is aided or perhaps rendered unnecessary when a principle, ethic, or rule so clearly defines the conduct we are after—conduct within reach of our current repertoire—that we are able to engage in it despite the pull of personal history; and aided further when it is clear that the benefits of engaging in the desired conduct far outweigh the benefits of not doing so. These tools—revisioning the past, holding fast to principle, arranging/understanding the consequences—allow us to replace degrees of historical inevitability with degrees of freedom. They give us leverage over a past that aims us in a direction we now consider problematic and so are tools that can serve us when we decide that what is needed is a change in direction or a new beginning.

6 It is also true that our desires, as well as our means for achieving them, can become distorted. We can come to desire things that we do not need, things that are in fact destructive. However, the assumption here is that at the deepest level, our desires are the same and are not destructive. Before contact with the potentially distorting influences of family, neighborhood, and/or society, the desire for fulfillment (the realization of inherent possibilities, wholeness, or full human maturity) already exists—a desire that runs the course of a lifetime. Each individual's behavior, though clumsy, selfish, and unenlightened, can be a calling out for that fulfillment. This may be fiction or hypothesis, but it is useful nonetheless, encouraging us to view ourselves (and others) as beings striving however unconsciously to realize our full development as persons.

7 See the work of Maria Nemeth (note 3 above). Also Hayes, *Get Out of Your Mind & Into Your Life*.

8 Schumacher, *A Guide for the Perplexed*, p. 72.

9 Ibid, pp. 72–74.

10 Hayes and his colleagues (see note 9 above) have developed numerous techniques for this purpose.

11 See also in this regard *The Sovereignty of Good* by Iris Murdoch (London: Routledge Classics, 2001, p. 82). Murdoch discusses the value of beauty as perceived through art and nature to clear the mind of self-obsessive thoughts: "I am looking out of my window in an anxious and resentful state of mind, oblivious of my surroundings, brooding perhaps on some damage done to my prestige. Then suddenly I observe a hovering kestrel. In a moment, everything is altered. The brooding self with its hurt vanity has disappeared. There is nothing now but kestrel. And when I return to

thinking of the other matter, it seems less important. And of course this is something which we may also do deliberately: give attention to nature in order to clear our minds of selfish care."

[12] Ibid, pp. 54–55. Murdock discusses the importance of one's "object of attention" in affecting behavior (or as is stated in the text, in "setting the occasion" for desired behavior): "It is also a psychological fact, and one of importance in moral philosophy, that we can all receive moral help by focusing our attention upon things which are valuable: virtuous people, great art, perhaps . . . the idea of goodness itself. Human beings are naturally 'attached,' and when an attachment seems painful or bad, it is most readily displaced by another attachment, which an attempt at attention can encourage. There is nothing odd or mystical about this, or about the fact that our ability to act well 'when the time comes' depends partly, perhaps largely, upon the quality of our habitual objects of attention." She then quotes the biblical passage from Philippians 4:8: "Whatsoever things are true, whatsoever things are honest, whatsoever things are just, whatsoever things are pure, whatsoever things are lovely, whatsoever things are of good report; if there be any virtue, and if there be any praise, think on these things."

[13] Hayes, *Get Out of Your Mind*, p. 10. For Hayes, the prospect of suffering is an inevitable byproduct of the fact that human beings have language and, thus, the capacity to think relationally. Humans can relate the most beautiful, joyful event to the absence of a loved one and suddenly the event becomes unbearably sad. Hayes argues that this capacity—to relate anything to anything—makes possible both remarkable problem-solving capacity and inevitable suffering. We are conscious of what and whom we have lost; conscious also of the discomfort, injustice, and injury we have seen and perhaps endured. And all of this is woven together with language, recall, our capacity to associate anything with anything, thus making suffering an almost certain part of human experience.

[14] Ibid, pp. 165–91.

[15] Ibid, pp. 7–8.

[16] Hayes and his colleagues have developed a number of techniques for viewing thoughts and separating oneself from the thoughts one thinks. These techniques are collectively known as defusion. "Cognitive defusion techniques . . ." writes Hayes, "help you make the distinction between the world as structured by your thoughts and thinking as an ongoing process. When your thoughts are about you yourself, defusion can help you to distinguish between the person doing the thinking and the verbal categories you apply to yourself through thinking," (Hayes, *Get Out of Your Mine*, p. 69). And again, "When you think a thought, it structures your world. When you

see a thought, you can still see how it structures your world (you understand what it means), but you also see that you are doing the structuring. That awareness gives you a little more room for flexibility" (p. 71).

17 Hayes, *Get Out of Your Mind*, pp. 153–54, 197.

18 Wilber, *A Brief History of Everything*, p. 139.

19 With the center of gravity concept in mind, it is possible to perhaps slightly expand what is typically thought of as the purpose of leadership. From the point of view of this book, the purpose of leadership is to raise the center of gravity. That is one of its duties. It is also one of the measures of good leadership. Whatever the organization (whether workplace, family, team, or society), the responsibility of leadership is to interact with the structures, components, processes, and individuals comprising the organization so as to raise the organization's center of gravity. However, it is not leadership's job alone. Or, to put it another way, whenever anyone in an organization behaves so as to raise the organization's center of gravity, leadership of a most fundamental sort is provided. The rise depicted in Figure 2 may have been the result of actions taken by formal leadership (the structure of the organization may have been revised, new practices adopted, the division of labor revamped, etc.). Still, at a deeper level, the rise occurred because leaders within the organization constructively responded to the challenges that came their way. The revising of the organization's structure, the adoption of new practices, the revamping of the division of labor, these may have been leadership's response to its dilemmas, issues that had to be faced if the organization was to evolve. Or the rising of the center of gravity shown in Figure 2 may have occurred or been assisted as individuals throughout the organization at whatever level chose on a slightly more frequent basis to ethically and creatively resolve their own dilemmas. In either case, leadership is exercised, with leadership of this sort available to all members of the organization.

Part V—*The Theater of Change*

1 Wilshire, *Role Playing and Identity,* pp. ix–x.

2 Augusto, *Games for Actors and Non-Actors*.

3 See the works of Virginia Satir, including *Conjoint Family Therapy* (Palo Alto, CA: Science and Behavior Books, 1983); *The New Peoplemaking* (Palo Alto, CA: Science and Behavior Books, 1988); *The Satir Model: Family Therapy and Beyond* (Palo Alto, CA: Science and Behavior Books, 1991).

4 The role-playing procedure follows a modification of Boal's model developed by

Douglas Paterson, Professor of Dramatic Arts at the University of Nebraska at Omaha.

[5] Wilshire, *Role Playing and Identity*, p. 11.

[6] Hillenbrand, Laura. *Seabiscuit: An American Legend*. New York: Random House, 2001, p. 106.

[7] Wilshire, *Role Playing and Identity*, p. 152: "It can be argued that it took philosophy over two thousand years, until Hegel, to reach this insight: a human being can become itself, its self, only when it makes its own what others have made of it." And again (p. 204): " . . . the life-actor like the stage actor must make his own to ever greater degrees what others have made of him."

[8] Mead, G. H. "A Behavioristic Account of the Significant Symbol." *Journal of Philosophy,* Vol. XIX, 1922. This appears as a footnote in Wilshire, *Role Playing and Identity*, p. 166.

[9] Quoted in Will Durant's *The Story of Philosophy: The Lives and Opinions of the World's Greatest Philosophers* (New York: Simon & Schuster, 1961, p. 312).

[10] In *The Denial of Death* (New York: The Free Press, 1973), Ernest Becker discusses what he calls "the neurotic type." His discussion emphasizes the developmental value implicit in not sitting back but, instead, overcoming the fear—risking, acting, turning the fool loose in small but meaningful ways for the cause of one's growth as a person. "The self arises in conduct," as Mead said (note 8). "To live," writes Becker, "is to engage in experience at least partly on the terms of the experience itself. One has to stick his neck out in the action without any guarantees about satisfaction or safety. One never knows how it will come out or how silly he will look, but the neurotic type wants these guarantees. He doesn't want to risk his self-image . . . Instead of living experience he (the neurotic) ideates it; instead of arranging it in action, he works it all out in his head" (p. 183).

[11] Wilshire, *Role Playing and Identity*, p. 253.

[12] This is not so of all cultures, of course. While all provide frameworks, each with its center of gravity, it can hardly be said that all fend off decay. Some hasten it. There is gang culture, for example; the culture of organized crime; the enabling culture; cultures that are racist, xenophobic, and oppressive. And while these cultures exist because they serve some need—from the need to belong to the need to survive—still it can be argued that they are born out of external conditions that are themselves distorted: extreme poverty, inequality, powerlessness, conditions that often contribute to ill-formed and unprepared personalities, conditions that result in cultures with a

limited ability to serve the long-term interests of their members. Here, however, as from the beginning of this book, the interest is in the development of cultures that do serve the long-term developmental interests of their members, cultures that support and do not damage the pursuit of inherent possibilities.

[13] I believe this phrase should be attributed to Urban, *Fundamentals of Ethics*.

[14] Fuller, R. Buckminster. *Critical Path*. New York: St. Martin's Press, 1981.

[15] Wright, Robert. *Nonzero: The Logic of Human Destiny*. New York: Vintage Books, 2000.

[16] Wilshire, *Role Playing and Identity*, p. 204: "One is returned to himself augmented, confirmed, and perhaps clarified by the other. One has left his mark on the other and through him upon oneself—l'effet c'est moi!—the effect, it is I!"

[17] Durant, Will and Ariel. *The Lessons of History*. New York: Simon and Schuster, 1968, p. 72.

[18] Schumacher, *A Guide for the Perplexed*, p. 139.

[19] Wilshire, *Role Playing and Identity*, p. xii.

[20] Wright, *Nonzero*, p. 135.

Afterword

[1] Urban, *Fundamentals of Ethics*, p. 225.